Foreword by Jeff York, Founder of Paycom

7 Ways
7 Times

Professional

SECOND EDITION

SELLING

IN THE 21ST CENTURY

JOHN DIETRICH & CARY NICHOLS

Kendall Hunt
publishing company

Kendall Hunt
publishing company

www.kendallhunt.com
Send all inquiries to:
4050 Westmark Drive
Dubuque, IA 52004-1840

Text only ISBN: 978-1-7924-0853-3
Text with GoReact ISBN: 978-1-7924-0852-6

Published in the United States of America

To Becky, Kielan, Maggie, and Bella: the discipline in which you approach your day
and the grit you deploy into every activity are truly admirable.
You have truly impacted the way I approach, teach, and coach professional sales.
This one's for you!

—JT

Kathy, to you, the greatest deal I ever closed, and to the two most spectacular ROI's we share.
Many wish for, yet few realize the amazing journey we live together every day.

Kath, Whit, Court, Thank You for your unwavering support through this experience—Clients for Life!

All My Love ~C~

BRIEF CONTENTS

CONTENTS

FOREWORD

Professor John Dietrich and Mr. Cary Nichols truly get it. And the "it" is professional selling! The students coming out of Arizona State University's professional sales program (many of them students in John's courses) are among the finest and most influential found on any college campus in the country. They have gone on to sell services, technology, chemicals, private jets, medical devices, consulting engagements, and pharmaceuticals—just to name a few. I have gotten to know many of these sales professionals, and some work directly with me at my company! The behaviors and skills that they are developing as they go through the sales program and take this class are the perfect recipe for entry into the twenty-first century sales force. These students are succeeding at an exponential rate in the business world because they are learning the foundation of professional sales, applying practical knowledge that can be used immediately, and experience that transcends most professions.

I have had the opportunity to not only review the contents of this textbook as the material was being developed, but to also speak and engage directly with the students coming out of their sales program. I can say—enthusiastically—that the chapters you are about to read and discuss in the classroom are the perfect foundation for a career in professional selling. With each turn of the page you will be taken on a journey from the "great body of experience" that John and Cary amassed during many successful years as high level professional executives. These stories are clearly written, highly engaging, and ultra-practical. You will likely begin deploying many of these sales tactics and techniques immediately.

Like John and Cary, I have a great passion for teaching young people the skills necessary to succeed in business. At Paycom we pride ourselves on hiring the very best sales professionals! To have had some helpful level of influence and effect on the life of an emerging executive is a great joy. Dietrich and Nichols carry that exact same passion, and with every turn of the page you will feel it, too. The authors have an innate ability to touch people's lives by teaching that professional selling is more than a career choice; it is an absolute necessity for anyone looking to succeed greatly in business and in their personal life.

Good Selling!

Jeff York
Chief Sales Officer, Paycom
http://www.paycom.com

PREFACE

BACKGROUND AND PHILOSOPHY

When the authors of this textbook first investigated the possibility of writing a "Professional Sales" book aimed at the undergraduate audience, they found two glaring opportunities: First, there is a great deal of text that offered theoretical concepts, but few that offered students the practical "how to put the concepts into practice." Second, just about every collegiate book they investigated focused solely on the concept of sales with respect to products or services, but almost always omits how sales (and selling principles) applies to ALL of our personal and professional lives as well. That's right—whether you are aware of this fact or not—every one of us is in the business of selling! We are ALL selling something regardless of the job description. **That means that every student taking this course has something to gain by engaging in these selling principles.**

Let us take these two observations one step further.

Most sales and marketing textbooks—particularly on the undergraduate level—will provide students an excellent understanding of what it means to build trust, prospect, close the deal and network. In *7 Ways 7 Times* the authors not only take the time to discuss the concepts, they also take the time to show every student taking the course "how" to put these behaviors and concepts into everyday practice. For example, building trust is the core foundation of any relationship—business or personal. If you are not sure exactly how to build trust with others, one way that you can start building trust with a customer—right now—is to commit to the principle of returning every phone call and every e-mail in the same business day that you received it. This is not a behavior that all who take this course will do. But it is one thing we all CAN do . . . if we choose to! When you return the e-mail or the phone call in the same business day that you received it you are demonstrating that you are reliable and trustworthy. Believe it or not, it's more common than you might think that sales representatives do not always return a customer call. In each chapter you will not only discuss the concepts, but you will see a variety of ways to practice the behaviors right now—today!

The second observation has to do with selling principles and how they apply to our personal lives. The term "sales" tends to have a negative connotation. So when most students hear "sales course" they naturally (but incorrectly) assume that this is not a course worth taking. But think about it: every job you ever apply for requires you to sell yourself to the hiring manager. Every boyfriend, girlfriend, spouse, club you join, or team you try out for requires that you put your best skills and behaviors forward. Here is a specific example that the authors highlight in the textbook on how to apply selling skills in your personal lives: joining a fraternity or sorority or club may seem intimidating at first. But what if you found out the club needed a graphics designer, or a person with events planning expertise, or excellent verbal and written skills? Assuming you have specific skills, you could leverage these skills and qualities in your application process. Instead of selling your popularity skills, consider asking the club President if they are seeking candidates who have specific qualities, skills, behaviors that will advance the mission of the club. Again, this is one way you could leverage selling skills in your personal lives.

And that is where the authors conceived the textbook's name: *7 Ways 7 Times*. In the authors' forty-plus years of combined selling experience, they have found that the path to success in sales cannot be boiled down to any one skill, behavior, or concept. There are a variety of ways and means to successfully market yourself. What works for you may not work for me, and so on!

This textbook is intended for students who seek to improve personally or professionally:

- ✓ Trustworthiness and Relatability
- ✓ Networking and Prospecting
- ✓ Effective Communication and Listening
- ✓ Understanding Buyers and Overcoming Objections
- ✓ Closing the Deal and Clients for Life

ORGANIZATION OF THE TEXTBOOK

To help instructors organize their course and roll out the concepts in a logical order, the textbook will be organized into three major categories:

Part One: Fundamentals of Building Relationships (Chapters 1–3)

Part One provides an overview of how relatability and trustworthiness are the foundations of successful selling and relationship building. For example, in Chapter 1 we discuss how a sales professional could be the smartest software sales rep in the country, but if I do not like you or trust you . . . I will not buy something from you. Therefore, we discuss the importance of established likeability, relatability, trustworthiness, and basic etiquette before "selling." These first three chapters provide a framework for the students to put fundamentals first and sales techniques second.

Part Two: Targeting Your Audience and Positioning (Chapters 4–6)

In Part Two students are exposed to real-world methods and processes for targeting a client, understanding how the client fits their business model, and then a variety of ways to publicly associate with the people we want to do business with. Students will learn clear distinctions between targeting the entire market versus targeting the top 20 prospects/customers they desire. A critical strategy in professional selling is to actively associate and engage with the people you want to do business with. The authors very specifically show students HOW to network, strategic ways to get involved in a business community, and how to communicate effectively once they are with clients.

Part Three: Closing the Deal (Chapters 7–11)

In Part Three the time has come to ask for the business—or—close the deal. We discuss a variety of ways that students can practice asking a client for their business. One of the most significant components of this section is learning to anticipate and deal with objections. The authors walk the students through a variety of techniques—particularly effective questioning methods—in dealing with customer objections. Students will then be exposed to the concept and behaviors associated with earning clients for life, and how profits and ROI actually increase as we keep customers in our portfolio.

Cases and/or Weekly Homework

At the end of every chapter is a case study for robust class discussion or homework assignment designed to isolate core concepts and challenge the students to take a position. Many of these cases do not have a particular right or wrong answer, nor are they designed that way. Each case and homework will require the students to call on their own set of sales capabilities and skill sets to solve the particular problem. While one student may suggest a conference call to gather information, another student may suggest a face-to-face meeting to drive home the concept of personal communication. In the real world, either of these approaches to business can work . . . and either of these approaches to business can fail. The students are required to take a position and defend their position with specific reasoning, intellect, and problem-solving skills.

Instructional Enhancements

The authors have placed an assignment at the very end of Chapter 11. The students will learn new ideas and techniques each week/chapter, and so the theory is that this final assignment will test their learning skills and abilities to absorb the collective concepts taught in this textbook. It is recommended that the instructors consider introducing this assignment at the very onset of the course and work with the students on a weekly basis to develop the curriculum and help the students bring it to fruition by the end of the course.

Lastly, more than seventy colleges from a variety of countries now compete with each other in role-play competitions. The two most notable role-play competitions are the National Collegiate Sales Competition (NCSC) and the International Collegiate Sales Competition (ICSC). These two sales competitions bring together the top collegiate sales programs in the United States and other countries to demonstrate their students' professional role-play and sales skills. Therefore, the authors of this textbook have decided to dedicate a portion of this textbook toward preparing students for these local, regional, national, and international sales competitions. Author John Dietrich led his sales team to fourth place at the 2015 ICSC sales competition. He also led his sales team to first place at the 2016 Liberty Mutual sales competition hosted by the University of Houston. His experience and insights on preparing and competing are shared in this textbook!

ABOUT THE AUTHORS

Courtesy John Dietrich

John Dietrich is a Lecturer of Marketing and Sales at Arizona State University (ASU) in Tempe, Arizona. In this capacity, Dietrich helps oversee the WP Carey School of Business' Sales Program, and currently teaches Sales Management and Sales Essentials. He is also a coach for ASU's traveling sales team, which ranked # 4 in the 2015 International Collegiate Sales Competition (ICSC), and # 9 (out of 80 universities) in the 2018 ICSC tournament. ASU also ranked # 1 at the 2018 Arizona Collegiate Sales Competition (ACSC) beating out 9 major universities. Dietrich holds an MBA and Masters of Management.

Courtesy Cary Nichols

Cary Nichols is a Strategic National Account Manager for ConvergeOne, an independent integrator of business communication, collaboration, and custom application solutions. Prior to joining ConvergeOne, Cary served as a Strategic National Sales Consultant in which he designed, managed, and deployed solutions for the global market. He managed a national territory with international presence serving Fortune 500 clients while maintaining 200 percent of quota year over year. Cary has been the recipient of the President's and Leadership Council from 2006–2019, and earned company-wide recognition for "Largest Single Deal in Company History over $38 million and recently the first and largest Cloud Managed Services deal."

Part One

Fundamentals of Building Relationships

CHAPTER 1
Trust and Relatability

Every morning in Africa, a gazelle wakes up, it knows it must outrun the fastest lion or it will be killed. Every morning in Africa, a lion wakes up. It knows it must run faster than the slowest gazelle, or it will starve. It doesn't matter whether you're the lion or a gazelle—when the sun comes up, you better start running.

— *African Proverb*

integrity

sincerity

Trust reliability

commitment

consistency

competence

CHAPTER OBJECTIVES

✓ Deepen your understanding of establishing, securing, and maintaining a long-term relationship

✓ Develop methods and tactics to earn trust with people

✓ Identify opportunities to relate to others and find commonalities with people

✓ Understand and appreciate the importance of credibility in the marketplace

✓ Deploy preparation as a discipline before every meeting

Professional Selling

the art of establishing a basic level of relatability and trust as a means to selling a service or a product to a customer.

Trust

the foundation in a relationship—business or personal—that enables the relationship to grow and develop.

When the authors of this book first sat down and discussed the art of professional selling, they quickly concluded that there is not one silver bullet or one particular behavior that sums up the making of a successful sales professional. The making of a successful sales professional is a combination of many things, executed over a long period of time, that are performed well! Approaching a client, partner, or any relationship (business or personal) may take an average of seven different ways, seven different times. For example, landing a $4 million account with a hospital will likely not happen in a single phone call. Earning a signed contract with a hospital may take one to two years, with a dozen meetings (some by phone, others in person), countless questions and details to be sorted out, and all managed by a professional sales representative who has earned the liking and trust of the hospital's doctors and administration. We will discuss more about positioning for a long-term relationship and the sales process in Chapter 8, but for now your ability to relate to people and build trust with the clients are the gateway to professional selling in the twenty-first century.

TRUST

Your ability to relate to another human being and earn trust is the foundation of any relationship—business or personal. You can be the smartest and most skilled car sales professional in the world, but if I don't trust you or don't like you . . . I am not buying a car from you. Let's take a closer look at trust.

ALTRUISM

LOYALTY

Relationship

DEPENDABILITY

CREDENTIALS

TRUTHFULNESS

Five Ways to Earn Trust in a Relationship

You could have a ten-year relationship with a customer, but if the trust between the two of you is violated, that relationship can be destroyed within seconds. And in your personal lives, whether it is a boyfriend, a friend, or a marriage, trust is the foundation that allows that relationship to grow.

So you may ask, "I'm a quiet person. I do not deal with people a whole lot. It's hard for me to build trust with people who I do not know." Whether you are, quiet, introverted, extroverted, a perfectionist, there are many ways you can help build trust with people, especially people you do not know that well. We have identified five ways for you to immediately begin practicing building trust in ANY relationship: business or personal.

Truthfulness is perhaps the easiest, most natural way of earning someone's trust. However, of the five ways to build trust discussed in this chapter, we have identified truthfulness as perhaps the most glaring disappointment in today's society.

As future leaders in our society it is important to note that the words you use should be aligned with your actions. A September 2016 Gallup poll asked the question: how much trust and confidence do you have in our federal government in Washington when it comes to handling national and international problems. Fifty percent of those polled said "not very much," or "none at all." That means that half of the country does not trust their elected leaders to get things done and improve the lives of everyday Americans. One of the most significant reasons for this distrust is that politicians do not always follow through with their promises and therefore appear to be untruthful.

> ### *Truthfulness*
>
> telling or expressing the truth in a candid manner that enables the recipient to make an honest, objective assessment of the situation.

One of the best things you can do when you make a mistake—in business or personal relationships—is to admit you made a mistake, and recognize that other people have been impacted by the mistake. People tend to empathize with truthfulness, honesty, candor, and straightforwardness. Let us consider two very similar, yet distinct scenarios:

SCENARIO 1: "Dad, I got a 70 percent on my test. It's my fault, I did not study and watched too much sports last weekend. I need to hit the books this week and pull that grade up."

©Monkey Business Images/Shutterstock.com

SCENARIO 2: "Dad, I got a 70 percent on my test. I'm so frustrated with this teacher. She is so mean to everybody, and she doesn't take time to explain things."

While either scenario is possible, the student in scenario one has an admirable honesty about himself/herself, and will likely have a father who is more understanding and more empathetic than in the second scenario. But notice how the student in scenario one did not just admit the shortfall, but also expressed how he/she would make the situation right? There is merit in turning a wrong into a right! If you dropped the ball, just tell people that . . . and then fix it. Most of us can empathize with mistakes because we have made similar missteps. But if you are not truthful when a mistake happens, the receiving party will respect you less, and trust will be impacted.

People do not tell the truth for many reasons: fear, posturing, manipulation, whatever the reason, people fail to see that telling the truth is an opportunity to demonstrate their character. Let's apply truth to a business situation found in the following ethical dilemma.

ETHICAL

Bob and Jeff have been friends for fifteen years. Both have had very successful careers, and have put some money aside. They have decided to open a family-friendly restaurant together. Prior to opening the restaurant they had a frank discussion on how they would treat very close friends and family when they come into the restaurant. Both had very good ideas on how to handle friends and family, but they agreed that giving free food and free drinks away are not in the best interest of a new business. Therefore, they agreed that all family and friends who come into the restaurant will have to pay their respective bill, although they will receive a VIP discount of 15 percent off their meal.

After the first three weeks of the business opening, Bob was working alone when his golf buddies came in for drinks after a long day on the golf course. After about an hour the friends stood up and signaled they were leaving. One friend said, "Bob, great seeing you. Do me a favor: I forgot my wallet. Take care of this bill for me, and the next time I see you I will pay you back! So sorry, but I promise I'll take care of it." The bill was only $65, but Bob knew he would probably not see these friends again for another month. And by then, it may be awkward asking for the $65 back. Bob then realized he did not have his wallet either, and therefore could NOT pay for his friends at this time. Bob recalled the deal he made with his business partner, Jeff: that all friends and family members must pay their bill. Small discount, but nothing for free!

Bob started to factor in that they only drank draft beer, and no inventory would be noticeably missing (such as beer bottles, which are easier for a business to track). The real loss to the business was approximately $12–$14 in actual costs to the business (the rest was mark-up, or "profit"). Since they were partners, half of that $12–$14 was Bob's anyway, so Jeff would only stand to personally lose $6–$7. And the reality was that Jeff would never find out. Bob also recalled that Jeff's son came in the other day to say hello, and he noticed that Jeff gave his son a free fountain soda while the son hung out. Bob never said anything to Jeff because fountain soda is only $0.99, and the real cost (or profit) to the business was maybe $0.12.

What should Bob do?

    A. Go ahead and comp the bill, move on. These situations are rare, and Jeff would never find out. It's not like Jeff pulled out $1 to pay for his son's soda.

    B. Put $14 in the register tomorrow. This way, the business did not lose money. Bob shouldn't have to pay the "profits" back to Jeff for customers who walked out without paying. This way, nobody loses.

    C. Tell Jeff the truth. Pay the $65 tomorrow. But also ask Jeff to put $1 back into the register for his son's soda.

    D. Pay the bill, but not bring up the $1 soda.

    E. None of the above. How would you handle it?

Dependability

consistency in a behavior, job duty, or personal responsibility that enables the receiving party to develop their trust with you.

Another way to earn trust is to be **dependable**. A big component of being dependable is to be consistent in your behavior. By developing a consistency in your behavior your business partners, customers, family members, and friends will eventually trust that aspect about you. If a working father comes home every day at 5:30 p.m. from work, the spouse and children will depend on this routine and plan some of their day around the consistent behavior. Dinner is easier to plan for the family, and helping the kids with homework and attending sporting events are behaviors the family will depend upon. On the other hand, if a working father is known for working late or stopping off with a few friends to play cards, the unpredictable behavior makes it more difficult for the family to plan family activities, dinner, sports activities, and even homework.

Same concept applies in business. If you tell a customer you will provide them an update on their loan every week, then make sure you call every week with that update (even if the update is: "I just wanted to let you know there has not been an update this week on your loan, but I will call you again next week with a loan status to see if anything changed."). It is acceptable to say that there is "nothing new." However, just because there is no action on the loan does not justify breaking your promise to the customer that you would call every week with an update. People who are dependable are consistent, and this is one way you can build trust with people.

Role Play

You are the boss of two employees. They have worked for you for five years. You are receiving a promotion and have been asked to pick your replacement:

- ✓ Employee A shows up every day on time, always has his/her work duties complete to perfection. However, he/she has a dull personality, rarely has anything to say to anybody, and can make it difficult

©ASDF_MEDIA/Shutterstock.com

to have fun at work because coworkers are not sure if he/she is offended by the extroverts at the office.

✓ Employee B is an employee you like a lot. They make the office a fun place to work, but admittedly all of the allotted sick days get used up every year, including a few unpaid days of absence. In fact, employee A is the one who makes up that extra work.

> Discuss amongst the class what attributes are more important to the business, the local office, and the customers.

Loyalty is another means of developing trust with a business professional or personal relationship. Loyalty enables you to give the benefit of the doubt to another person. The person receiving this loyalty will appreciate the fact that you will stand by them in the good times and the bad. Trust will grow because they know they can count on you for support. Think about it like this: you have banked at ABC bank for three years, and for the first time you accidentally bounced a check. In most banks, you likely will have incurred a significant fee. However, if the bank views you as a loyal customer who has not bounced a check in three years, they will likely give you the benefit of the doubt and waive the fee. The opportunity for the banker here is to tell the customer: "You can bank anywhere you want, but you have stayed with us for three years. I am certain this was just a mistake, and we will not charge a loyal customer like you a fee."

Same goes for your friends. They may come to you and confide that they are in a personal jam and need your help. Depending on the significance of the situation, you have a moment here to express your loyalty to that friend— without judging if they deserve this mess or not. Loyalty is an excellent way to build trust.

A well-known law firm that has experienced attorneys with admirable **credentials** can project a sense of trust immediately between a client and an attorney. We all know some extremely smart people, but if they do not have their Medical Doctorate (MD), we do not want them operating on us.

This is a challenge for the professional selling community (at large), because many professional sales agents are not required to have a professional designation. The mortgage crisis of 2008–2010 exposed a glaring problem in the banking community. While the vast majority of mortgage professionals were honorable and ethical people, the lack of professional credentials, ethics training, and oversight allowed far too many unscrupulous lenders into the lending business. It was not until recently that mortgage originators must register with the financial industry and receive mandatory minimal levels of training and secure professional credentials.

Loyalty

extending the benefit of the doubt to your business associates or personal relationships.

Credentials

having the proper education, experience, and/or expertise that demonstrate your relevant qualifications.

Obtaining the proper and requisite credentials is one way you build trust in a relationship.

Altruism

We have all heard the term "servant leader." When I think of a fireman, or a police officer, or paramedic, the word "unselfish" comes immediately to mind. The scene of a fireman running into a burning building has a deeply profound meaning in our society: these professionals are running TO the problem! But here is something to think about: generally speaking, society "loves" and/or "admires" first responders. Yet, each one of us reading this book has put out symbolic fires in our personal and/or professional lives. So it begs the question—how come first responders are loved and/or admired, but when the average person puts out a symbolic fire he/she is liked—at best? One is loved, the other liked. Here is some insight into why that may be the case: first responders do four things simultaneously really, really well. (1) First responders run to the problem. No matter how bad the situation is they

are coming in to fix it; (2) They don't point fingers or blame anybody as they are putting out the fire or resolving the issue at hand (even to the very people who may have started the fire or caused the problem to begin with!). Today is about solving the issue at hand, and there will be plenty of time later on to point fingers or figure out the root cause of what happened; (3) They don't complain. Have you ever heard of a fireman stop halfway up the staircase and say, "Hey, it's kind of hot in here. I need a break"? And, (4) to the first responder . . . this is what they signed up for. Their mentality is to get the job done and resolve the issue at hand.

©Gorodenkoff/Shutterstock.com

Most sales professionals run to the problem (item #1). They want to take care of their customers and remedy the problem. But sometimes professionals fall short on items 2–4 listed above: we can find ourselves blaming others, we tend to complain, and our mind-set can sometimes default to "this is not what I signed up for." From the authors perspective, executing on ALL four simultaneously is one way to adopt the "first-responder mentality," and we can almost guarantee your customers will admire these qualities about you!

In business, mistakes will happen, and there will be days your customers will be extremely mad or frustrated. Developing a sense of empathy or unselfishness will help you run to the problem and save the day. It's human nature to want to point the finger, blame someone else, or avoid responsibility. But it's also selfish to put yourself first before the customer. For example, if you are a professional sales representative with customers buying from your website, do not blame the delivery truck for failing to deliver the package. The customer believed YOU when they paid money and the package was shipped. Take responsibility for the package not arriving. Make the delivery truck failure YOUR problem—not the customer's—and run to the problem. If you take responsibility, empathize with the customer's frustration, and fix the problem, you will earn trust!

Many undergraduate students or young professionals find themselves working in restaurants or retail (among other industries). In these situations you may find that you took the customer's food order in a restaurant, but the kitchen made a mistake and cooked the wrong food. Too often we see waiters blame the kitchen or the busy staff. And too often the customer doesn't feel you completely understand or empathize with their frustration. Let's look at two possible responses to the customer:

1. "I am so sorry that we brought you the wrong food. The manager is aware of it, and we are recooking the meal right now. Your meal will be out in approximately eleven minutes, and this time it will be excellent. May I bring you a salad, new drink, or something to hold you over?"

2. "I am so sorry, the kitchen screwed up the order. We are just slammed tonight, and we will get it out to you as soon as we can."

Which of these two professionals ran to the fire? Better yet, if you OWNED the restaurant (or if you go into sales management and are entrusted with training sales professionals), which employee would you want handling the situation? In scenario A the professional put the customer's interest BEFORE their own, taking complete responsibility (and offered a specific solution to the problem).

✓ The message sent to the customer? "You are MY customer, and I take full responsibility for what happened. No excuses. Here's exactly how we will make it right. Here's what you can expect. And in the meantime here is what we will do to make your experience a better one."

In scenario B notice how the professional put his/her own interest BEFORE the customer's interest (and offered a vague solution to the problem).

✓ The message sent to the customer? "Not my fault. Someone else's fault. Your food will eventually get out to you."

What kind of professional are you? How do you want to be perceived by your customers, or your boss, or . . . your family? Do you make excuses? Or do you empathize and put the needs of others before your own? Being unselfish is another method you can incorporate when building trust.

As undergraduate students getting ready to begin your corporate careers, there is no better time than right now to practice these trust builders. Many of you already are very trustworthy people and execute these principles well.

Practice these five trust builders with your friends, your teachers, and your customers. You will see a noticeable uptick in how much they respect you . . . and trust you! The world needs trustworthiness now more than ever before.

LEVELS OF TRUST

We deal with many, many people in our lifetime. For purposes of this book we would like to focus on the people/entities that are the most critical: your family, your career, and your network (business friends or personal friends).

The two levels of trust that we will focus on are: transactional/moderate and going deep.

Transactional Level of Trust

The **transactional level of trust** is the basic level of a relationship that we come to expect between our neighbors, friends, business colleagues, and network. At this level, minimal expectations of honesty, dependability, loyalty, credentials, and altruism are needed in order to have a healthy relationship. For example, having a good relationship with your neighbor is important, and it is a relationship that you may depend on for various reasons (i.e., being a good neighbor, we may need their help on occasion). In these relationships you tend to react to each other: for example, you do not talk to the neighbors a whole lot, but they may need a favor from you every once in awhile. As a good neighbor you are happy to provide that favor. Minimal effort is required to establish a general level of trust, relatability, and even help each other on occasion. In most situations you may be "neighborly" for many years, but the relationship never evolves into you being the best of friends. That's OK, and very normal! In life not all of your neighbors will be your "best of friends."

Perhaps your neighbors ask you to take out their garbage while they are on vacation in California. You are reacting by saying yes.

> **Transactional Level of Trust**
>
> a lower level of trust that typically requires a reactive approach to the relationship; a minimal level of effort to earn and maintain. The repercussions of losing trust at the transactional level are less severe.

©Iakov Filimonov/Shutterstock.com

And they are "depending" on you to get this done. Such a situation requires a minimal level of relationship building or trust. However, if you forget to take out the garbage on Wednesday as you promised, they will likely be disappointed. But since the relationship is at the transactional level they may not make a big deal out of your omission. Since these relationships are generally transactional in nature, the neighbors will likely brush it off and tell you not to worry about it. You do not put much into the relationship, but you do not get a lot out of the relationship either.

Transactional relationships are reactive in nature, and require minimal effort to maintain. But let us now shift to more serious and deeper relationships: family and business.

Going Deep

Your family and career are not just important to your livelihood, they are critical! These are relationships you must protect, and they require maximum effort to earn, maintain, and grow. They call for proactive fundamentals of trust building. In business if a professional sales representative would like to deepen the relationship with his/her client, a proactive effort should be deployed.

Consider these two scenarios:

SCENARIO 1: Bob calls his bank and asks for new checks to be ordered and sent to his house. The banker reacts and takes care of the customer's check order. Five days later the new checks arrive at the customer's house. The customer is "content" but really ANY bank could have responded to these needs.

Now let's consider scenario 2, in which a banker wants to go deeper with his/her customers, and wants "customers for life!" The banker decides to make a proactive effort at the relationship in an effort to go above and beyond.

SCENARIO 2: The banker calls Bob a week later and says, "Hello Bob! It's JT down at the bank. I just wanted to check in and make sure you received those checks in the mail as promised. And, I wanted to see if there is ANYTHING else we could do for you Bob . . . "

Bob would appreciate the proactive call, especially if the checks never arrived as promised! But let's assume the checks DID arrive on time as promised. Bob might say, "Yes JT, I got the checks. And no, I do not need anything else. Thank you! But while I have you on the phone . . . do you happen to know the home loan rates these days?"

The banker's proactive behavior and efforts at growing the relationship will lead to customers for life.

Going Deep
Level of Trust

the highest level of trust that is required in a proactive approach to the relationship; requires maximum effort and time to earn, maintain, and grow. The repercussions of losing trust at the Going Deep level is severe.

One last distinction to make: when you reach a "deep" relationship with a customer, you are likely to maintain that customer if you made an honest mistake. For example, let's assume you called Bob to ensure he received his checks, but learned the checks never arrived. By taking a proactive approach and going deep with Bob, you have the ability to apologize, cancel the old checks, and order new checks immediately. However, by taking a transactional approach to Bob, you may never have learned that his checks got lost or stolen. The customer may lose trust in your bank, switch to a competing bank, and you may never know it!

EXERCISE

TRANSACTIONAL RELATIONSHIPS AND GOING DEEP

Next time you have a paper due, send the paper in a few days early and ask the professor "I know this is not due until Friday, but would you be comfortable taking a look to see if it hits the mark, and if you have any suggestions for me to improve it?"

You will notice that this proactive behavior will LIKELY increase your chances at getting a much better grade on the paper. If the professor says it hits the mark and makes a few suggestions to improve it (and let's assume you incorporate those suggested edits), you have just made it very difficult for them to give you a C on the paper. The professor will LIKELY appreciate your people skills and proactive approach to the course. It's another way to deepen the relationship with your professors and to develop trust with key faculty.

"Your customers aren't customers anymore. Your vendors aren't vendors anymore. They're either your teammates or someone else's teammates. If you're not on their team, they'll find someone who is."

—John Ellis

INTRODUCTION ON RELATABILITY

Being relatable is what sets the stage for trust. Put simply, your ability to sell—professional or personal—could be greatly diminished without the skill set to relate to someone and ultimately earn their trust. You may trust your spouse, but if you cannot relate to each other and find commonalities, the path may prove to be a difficult one. On the flipside, you can get along wonderfully, have much in common, and have the best time together. But if trust is violated, the path may prove to be a difficult one.

Therefore, as authors we concluded that trust and relatability/likeability would serve as the foundation of this textbook, and the launching pad into all of the other professional selling skills outlined in this textbook. Let us be clear, all of us are selling *something* in our personal and professional journeys. The same skills that enable us to (a) locate a customer, (b) make a sale to that customer, (c) maintain the relationship with that customer, and (d) make them customers for a lifetime are the SAME skills that we apply to our teammates, fraternities, sororities, clubs, friends, families, neighbors, and significant others. Each and every day we find ourselves selling something. And whether you are someone I want to work with at the office, a friend down the hallway whom I want to join a sorority with, or a person who I want to go out to dinner with (personal or professional), the art of selling and the skills required are intimately part of the process.

In relationships, trust and relatability are keys to achieving your long-term "common" goals. Therefore, for the purpose of this textbook, trust and relatability/likeability are considered mutually exclusive and foundational cornerstones for any team, any sport, or any business deal. Is it possible for a talented sports team to be successful if they did not trust one another, or lacked the basic ability to get along and relate to one other? It is possible, but no coach, no business manager, and no teammate welcomes such a situation. The potential for failure significantly escalates when teammates cannot relate to each other, or when there is mistrust.

> ### *Relatability*
> the commonalities of two persons or more that enable immediate rapport and relationship building.

WAYS TO BECOME RELATABLE AND LIKEABLE

So how do we become relatable? Some may think "I'm too quiet, I do not relate to people all that well." Others may say, "I am an extrovert, but I can sometimes come across as disingenuous." And then there are people in the middle who may say, "I don't care about anything except this team succeeding." Each of these personalities—and EVERY type of personality—has the capability of being relatable! Quiet, loud, perfectionist, funny, hard worker, diplomat, compassionate, conservative, risky, nerd, C-student . . . regardless of which one of these attributes reflects your style—YOU can turn ANY of these into an advantage for yourself and actually use it to be "relatable."

©vectorfushionart/Shutterstock.com

CASE DISCUSSION

One week before rush week, freshman Steve Johnson is considering joining ABC fraternity. The ABC's are one of the largest and most respected fraternities on campus. Steve is a quiet guy, keeps to himself, and is not one to be flashy. Furthermore, he has a dry sense of humor and can often appear to be bored and not having a good time. But he's also a huge college football fan and has developed advanced graphics design skills. He has an amazing knack for creative artwork and website design. He was also the captain of his high school track team.

Later on that day, Steve attends his lab class and realizes that he is sitting next to Johnny Batton, President of ABC Fraternity. Johnny leans over and introduces himself, and says, "This is such an awesome week. We will be recruiting new pledges into our fraternity. But we don't want any deadbeats! We want new brothers who will help this fraternity remain great—long after I am gone. Yes, we know how to have a good time. But we also are very competitive in sports and do a lot of good charity around campus. I am proud of our brothers and what we accomplish as a fraternity."

Steve couldn't believe he was sitting next to the President. This was a club he really wanted to be associated with. So he just smiled and listened, not sure exactly how to respond to Johnny's enthusiasm or charisma. He also became privately discouraged after hearing "We don't want any deadbeats."

1. Does Steve have an opportunity to be relatable? Or does his quiet nature preclude him from trying?

2. What "specific" professional selling advice would you recommend to Steve in this moment?

3. Should Steve leave it alone and wait for rush week to officially begin? Or is now an opportune time?

Students find themselves in similar situations like this all of the time. Whether it is a fraternity rush week or a career fair, the selling opportunity is the exact same. Both entities are looking for men and women who will make profound contributions and add immediate value. In the case above, although Steve is quiet by nature he has many skills and talents to offer the ABC fraternity.

The difference between a professional sales representative and an ordinary person (such as Steve) is that a professional sales representative recognizes the opportunity and immediately calibrates his relatability factor. A professional sales representative has a symbolic toolbox filled with relatability tools. Each of us has a lifelong set of experiences and talents that we can draw upon. For example, if the potential client likes football, then talk football when you meet! If the potential buyer is more information driven, then keep the conversation factual and to the point.

In the fraternity case above, Steve has the opportunity to be relatable, but it is incumbent upon him to spot the opportunity and connect the dots with the fraternity president. Here are a couple ways Steve can be relatable:

1. "Johnny, I have been eyeing your fraternity for the past two weeks. Are you guys looking for new brothers who are graphics designers and who develop websites?"

2. "That's awesome, Johnny. You guys sound like you have the full package. Is there room in your fraternity for athletes who ran track in high school and love football?"

3. "My name is Steve, and one of the things that attracts me to your fraternity is your charitable arm and desire to improve lives around campus. I have talents and skills that could advance your fraternity's charitable arm and really make a difference on campus."

Steve may be quiet. However, being relatable in this moment does not require a ton of effort, but rather an awareness of your strengths and what you bring to the relationship. When you know your target audience (business or personal) each one of us has SOMETHING we can relate to the receiving party.

Sales professionals are rarely caught off guard because they know their target audience. They do their homework. They know their audience. They actively seek opportunities to relate and build trust. When they are engaging a customer, they look for an opening in the conversation to offer value and connect the dots. They are prepared to have a relevant conversation on a moment's notice. In the case of Steve and Johnny above, all Steve had to do was list what he is good at, and then wait for the opportunity to speak with the fraternity. You do not need to be an extrovert to do this. Preparation is all that is needed.

STUDENT EXERCISE

It is now time to discuss the semester long project that will include many of the concepts discussed in the coming chapters. Your teacher will refer to the assignment found at the back of Chapter 11 and begin breaking the class into groups of 4–10 (depending on class size). Once the teams are formed, one student should serve as the team captain/leader. The project is a semester long and the instructor will work with the class to allot a sufficient amount of time for preparation, discussion, and ultimately an excellent final product. Please see Chapter 11 Homework for details! Good luck.

HOW TO PREPARE

We just discussed various ways to be relatable and connect with others. But what happens when you are seeking a job, or going blindly to an interview, or randomly have a customer show up in your office? Sometimes being relatable warrants more specified preparation and due diligence. There are a couple of recommended methods of approaching complex meetings.

First, know the situation you are walking into. Whether it is a job interview or a customer who has unique needs, a good habit to develop is to review in advance the job requirements or business expectations of your customer. Then pencil down your strengths that compliment those business needs. For example, perhaps the job description is seeking candidates who possess:

- ✓ strong presentation skills,

- ✓ excellent communication tactics, and

- ✓ demonstrable interdepartmental collaboration.

For your job interview, it is strongly recommended to be aware of what they expect and how you can meet those expectations. As an undergraduate student or young sales professional, your career may be limited but your transferrable skills are not. Sports teams, waiting tables, fraternities and sororities, and university clubs are all opportunities to develop skills and relate to business needs. Let's consider a student who has previously waited tables and would like to articulate how their skills as a waiter match the skills needed for a customer service representative position.

SCENARIO 1 (in a job interview): "I waited tables and this was great experience. My duties included taking orders, collaborating with the kitchen, and providing excellent customer service, and managing money."

SCENARIO 2 (in a job interview): "My job as a waiter provided an excellent opportunity to develop my presentation and communication skills. I had to approach people from all walks of life, listen to their needs, and work with other departments to ensure the customers had an excellent experience."

In scenario 1 the student truly misses an opportunity to connect the dots and convince the hiring manager that waiting tables was an excellent foundation for customer service. However, notice how in scenario 2 the student is articulating transferrable skills that match the needs of—for example—a customer service representative position. Scenario 2 demonstrates reliability, listening, and enhancing the customer experience.

Additionally, if you were in a fraternity or sorority, write down exactly how coordination between members of your club and the Interfraternity Council (IFC) required professional presentation skills, clear communication, and the ability to work in cohesion with various organizations on campus. If you are on a sports team, write down exactly how working with others, putting the team first, executing strategy, and working with various coaches enhanced your communication and interdepartmental skill sets. By knowing the situation and expectations of your audience, you have the opportunity to be relatable to the interviewer and his/her company.

Second, know the person you are scheduled to meet. Many times you have the opportunity to know in advance who you are about to meet. In the days of social media and the World Wide Web, there are many ways to find out information about the person you are meeting. LinkedIn is a terrific method of finding out someone's title, experience, education, clubs they affiliate with, career path, hometown, awards, and much more. Basic preparation on the person you are meeting will dramatically increase your ability to build rapport, get the conversation started, and allow you to relate!

CHAPTER SUMMARY

The foundation of professional selling is being relatable and earning trust. These are inextricable and critical to earning, developing, and maintaining a relationship. If I like you, but do not trust you . . . the relationship will likely struggle. If I trust you, but do not like you . . . the relationship will likely struggle. We cannot relate and build trust with every human being in the world, but we can take proactive steps to increase our chances with each person. There are many ways to earn trust. Truthfulness, dependability, loyalty, credentials, and altruism are five ways you can actually start using today, if you have not already! Your ability to relate to another person is not limited. Being quiet, slow, loud, annoying, introverted, are not good excuses to avoid career fairs, social clubs, or asking someone out on a date. Awareness of your strengths and preparation for your meetings are a powerful antidote for quiet or shy! Each of us can be relatable!

REFERENCE

Gallup Poll. http://news.gallup.com/poll/5392/trust-government.aspx

1

HOMEWORK

Ben was ecstatic. He just sold eight new ultrasound machines to the local hospital. Such a sale signified he would likely place in the President's Top 10 list for the quarter, and he would receive a very handsome commission check to reward his sale. The following month Ben received a phone call from the hospital's Vice President of Procurement, and here is how the conversation went:

VP PROCUREMENT: "Ben. Good morning. Do you have fifteen minutes to talk?"

BEN: "Jack! Thanks for the call. Yes, of course I have time. How can I help you?"

VP PROCUREMENT: "Well, the eight ultrasound machines we purchased were supposed to arrive yesterday. Instead, three arrived yesterday, two showed up today. We are missing three ultrasound machines. Additionally, I am a little frustrated. I was hesitant to place this order with you because we had the same problems five years ago with the last representative from your company. You promised that you would be here with me as these machines arrived yesterday. Not only did you not show up to assist myself and our doctors with questions they had about the new machines, but the order is incomplete! I need my other three machines, and I need you here helping our doctors get acclimated with the machines."

Ben completely forgot about his promise to show up at the hospital yesterday. But still, in his mind there was no reason for all eight ultrasound machines to not show up. At least if the machines showed up as promised, his only fault would be failing to be present. Receiving five machines was unacceptable. To make matters worse, it was 11 a.m. on Thursday and he already took paid time off for the balance of the weekend to rent a pontoon with his five best friends who were in town visiting him.

QUESTION 1: There are three other reps from Ben's company who perform similar sales. Is it acceptable for Ben to guarantee the remaining three machines get delivered today, but for one of his colleagues to fill in for him at the hospital to answer questions from the doctors? What additional risks does Ben have by sending one of his colleagues to the hospital to answer questions?

QUESTION 2: Is there merit in Ben's reasoning that him failing to show up was not as significant as the missing three ultrasound machines?

CHAPTER 2
Listening

It's Not What You Say, It's What People Hear.

— *Frank Luntz*

CHAPTER OBJECTIVES

✓ To develop a deeper awareness and understanding of listening not just with your ears, but your eyes, mind, and body

✓ To understand the meaning of active listening

✓ To understand the importance of listening in relationship building

✓ To explore five new ways to sharpen your listening skills and immediately improve your personal and business relationships

LISTENING

Chapter 1 laid an excellent foundation for each of you to not only begin a relationship, but also methods to develop and maintain that relationship for a lifetime. In this chapter we will focus on **listening** as a requisite skill in the relationship building process.

Listening

the process of how the recipient in a conversation receives information through his/her ears, eyes, mind, and body in an effort to respond objectively.

In 2006 a young, moderately successful mortgage loan officer named JT sat dejected as he looked at the phone. The young banker just got off the phone with the former CEO of one of the largest private banks in the United States, and this CEO just called to say he will NOT be originating a loan with JT. Instead, the former CEO decided to go with a competitor across town. JT sat dejected because a $400,000 home loan just slipped through his hands. To make matters worse, the loan went to the competition. JT wanted this loan not only for the volume, but for the potential referrals that a wealthy executive could send his way if the loan was executed properly.

Taking out a pen and paper, JT decided to take inventory of why he lost this loan.

Twenty-four hours earlier, JT and the former CEO sat in the banker's office discussing the executive's beautiful new home.

JT: "What's your financial objective with this loan?"

CEO: "JT, I want the lowest possible interest rate, and I am interested in the Adjustable Rate Mortgage (ARM) loans that many of my friends seem to be so fond of."

©Blue Planet Studio//Shutterstock.com

JT: "It is true ARM loans have lower rates than traditional 30-, 15-, and 10-year fixed loans, but the rate is only guaranteed for the first 3 years; whereas, the traditional 30-, 15-, and 10-year loans are only slightly higher interest rates, and guaranteed for the entire life of the loan. If you go the ARM route, there is a chance the interest rate could potentially jump 2%. Why not take the safer, more traditional route and not worry about this ever again?"

CEO: "JT, thanks for the advice, but I will make a lot more money with the savings from the lower rate as I plan on investing those savings in the financial market. And in three years, if the home loan rates jump, I have the financial means to pay off my home loan in full. So my goal—right now—is to get the lowest possible rates and revisit the loan in three years when the current lower rate expires."

JT shook the former CEO's hand and said he will take a look at a few options and give him a call in a couple hours. As he sat in the office reviewing home loan options, JT could not help recall doing ARM loans for customers in the past. After the introductory period, many of the customers saw their rates rise to uncomfortable levels, forcing them to refinance and lock into longer-term loans. Some customers even vented that a "good" banker would have talked them out of the shorter term loan and into the life-long fixed rates that traditional loans usually offer. Some customers did not appreciate—nor understand—why they had to refinance out of an ARM loan and back into a traditional fixed loan, paying thousands of dollars in closing costs all over again. Yep, JT has seen this a few times before and decided to give the former CEO a call and try to get him to see the "big picture." JT picks up the phone and dials the former executive's cell phone number. After a few pleasantries were exchanged, the call went like this:

JT: "Ok, so I did some digging. I can get you into a 3/1 ARM loan with a rate of 4.5%. This rate is only guaranteed for three years, and it may fluctuate drastically each year after. I am having heartburn offering you this ARM loan, because I can lock your home loan in for 30 years, guaranteed at 5%. For a 1/2% difference, I believe you are making a mistake. I would like you to reconsider the 30-year locked rate."

CEO: "Thank you JT for your efforts. But it is clear you are not listening to me. I am a former bank CEO and I understand the risk and reward of finance. My financial planners have earned me a yearly average of 15% profits with my investments. With a lower interest rate on my home loan—even for just three years—I would be able to invest those savings in the market and gain a healthy return in the thousands each year. I told you earlier that in three years—if the home loan rates jump higher—I have the financial means at my disposal to pay off the loan and re-evaluate my financial circumstances at that time. I appreciate what you would like to see happen, but this is my money, and my goals. I need a banker who will understand my short- and long-term financial goals. I think I am going to go with my brother's mortgage banker downtown. Thanks for your time, JT."

One of the most common questions sales professionals receive from undergraduate students is: "What is the most common mistake or challenge that professional sales representatives make?" After decades of professional selling, managing, and coaching the answer is actually simple: we talk too much, and we don't truly listen. In the story above, JT failed to listen to his customer. Or, at least the customer felt he was not being "heard." Naturally, many of us tend to believe we are good listeners, but the research is overwhelmingly to the contrary—particularly in business. For example, the American Management Association did a study in which they found that 56 percent of respondents believe that their management team does not do an acceptable job of listening to their concerns.

To send the message that you are truly listening to another person, it is recommended to do so with more than just your ears. True listening occurs when a person's ears, eyes, mind, and body are 100 percent focused on the person speaking. Let's discuss each of these four components of listening.

©Dean Drobot/Shutterstock.com

1. Listening with the ears:

Now let's imagine you walk in to the boss's office, she is fiercely typing and has a tense look on her face as she stares at her computer. "Hi Bob," she says in a plain tone as she continues to type, "Come on in. Just getting this report done for the CEO. What's up?" As you make your way to the empty chair across from her desk it becomes apparent that she is listening, but something more urgent has her mind, eyes, and body. You appreciate the open-door policy, but you make your statement quick and tell her you'll swing back a little later. "That's awesome, Bob. Thank you. And good work!" she says as you walk out. The boss heard you, and she is likely very pleased that her project has been completed. But the message sent to the employee is something more important is happening, and therefore enthusiasm in the room is greatly reduced.

2. Listening (or NOT listening) with the eyes:

It's Friday and the deadline for your project has been met. Excited, you walk into your boss's office and are poised to tell her the good news. As you enter she stands up, smiles, shakes your hand, closes the door, and then asks you to sit down at her desk. The boss says, "Hello Bob! I am so glad to see you. So what's going on?" Right as you are about to inform her of the good news, you notice she reaches onto her desk and picks up her cell phone, types in something quickly, and then begins to scroll the cell phone with her thumb. "We finished our project, and my team is so excited," you say. Ms. Swenson is nodding and smiling, but continues to stare at her cell. She looks up at you for a second and says, "That's great. I would love to see it later on today." Within a couple seconds she looks back at her cell phone and begins scrolling again. In this situation, the boss demonstrated some basic listening skills and even some active listening skills (nodding as you delivered good news). But her eyes were focused on her cell phone, and this can send a message to employees that she was listening but distracted with something else.

3. Listening (or not listening) with the mind:

It's Friday and you cannot wait to tell the boss about how your department pulled together and met the deadline for the marketing plan. Excited, you walk in to Ms. Swenson's office and say, "I have terrific news Ms. Swenson, do you have a minute?" She stands up, smiles, and walks over to shut the door. "Of course I do Bob, let's hear it. Come on over and grab a seat." As you begin telling her how the team finished up the project today at noon, Ms. Swenson reaches into her purse and pulls out lipstick and a small pocket mirror. She freshens up as you talk, and in a few seconds she puts the kit back into her purse. You finish the good news and she smiles at you and says, "This is great! When do you think you will have it finished by Bob?" As her subordinate, you become awkward and dejected. Awkward because you just explained that the project was complete, but she spent the time fixing herself up in a mirror. Dejected because this was a big win for your department, and it warranted the full attention of the department manager. Clearly she "heard" what you said, and even acknowledged that something special was happening. But the signal she sent to her employee is that she was not completely listening and her mind was somewhere else.

4. Listening (or not listening) with the body:

There are people who will listen with the ears, eyes, and mind, but their body language tells a completely different story. The previous three scenarios applied to a business setting. Let's apply body language to a personal setting. Your eighteen-year-old daughter brings home a boyfriend she met at college. Excited, she walks in and announces that this is Chuck, and he is a freshman at the same college she attends. The wife comes out from another room, shakes his hand, and says, "Hi Chuck, so nice to meet you. Can I get you something to drink? Come on in and make yourself at home." The father is also happy to meet Chuck, but is laying on the couch and too lazy to get up. He makes eye contact with the young man, and yells out, "Hi Chuck!" but never gets off the couch to shake his hand. Chuck nods and waves to the father, and then simply walks toward the mother and says he would love a glass of water. The father's body language of laying on the couch and not moving gives the impression to his daughter that Chuck is not important; whereas, the mother gave her full attention to her daughter's excited announcement.

5. *Listening with the eyes, ears, mind, and body:*

In each of the previous four scenarios an argument can be made that he/she is listening, even though their eyes are looking elsewhere or their body language expresses disinterest. But now let's discuss a scenario in which listening occurs with the ears, eyes, mind, and body. Imagine you walk into your boss's office with the intention of delivering the fantastic news. Upon walking in, the boss turns to you and says, "Bob! How in the world are you today? Come on over here, sit down. What brings you in today?" Upon sitting down you look across the desk and notice that your boss, Ms. Swenson has closed the office door, sits down and minimizes her computer screen, crosses her legs, folds her hands, and with a big, bright smile looks at you and says, "I am so glad you came in. So what's on your mind?"

In this situation, your fantastic news is likely to be received by the boss with enthusiasm because your boss has made it crystal clear—with her ears, eyes, mind, and body language—that you are the most important thing in the room right now. She wants nothing to distract or take away from your great news.

DID YOU KNOW . . .

1. Average person talks at a rate of about 125–175 words per minute (Carver, Johnson, and Friedman 1970)

2. Average person can listen at a rate of up to 450 words per minute (Carver, Johnson, and Friedman 1970)

3. Average student forgets 33%–50% of short talks by faculty members within 8 hours (Nichols and Stevens, 1957)

Active Listening

the deliberate application of verbal and/or non-verbal methods in order for the receiver in a conversation to optimize the reception, interpretation, evaluation, and ultimate response to the sender in a conversation.

Active Listening is a highly recommended listening skill to use in an important conversation. Active Listening signifies the deliberate application of verbal and/or non-verbal methods in order for the receiver in a conversation to optimize the reception, interpretation, evaluation, and ultimate response to the sender in a conversation (Steil, Baker, Watson 1983).

The differentiating factor in Listening versus Active Listening is the level of concentration the receiver applies to the conversation. We will discuss concentration as a skill later in the chapter, but for Active Listening purposes concentration is what permits the receiver to minimize distractions and consciously contribute to the conversation by leveraging advanced listening skills. For example, in a quarterly review a manager may list out two to three areas of improvement for his/her employee. The employee can either sit there and listen attentively without saying a word—or—the employee can take an active listening approach such as nodding their head in agreement and potentially repeating back what they heard from the boss: "So you believe that if I work on my customer retention rate that I could possibly place in the top 10 next year?"

In this situation there is not necessarily a wrong or right, but rather which listening skill would be more effective to deploy. It's never easy for a manager to provide constructive criticism to his/her employees. If an employee simply sits with their hands folded and listens to the manager without moving or saying much, the manager may feel the employee is embarrassed and possibly a little defensive. However, when the employee takes an Active Listening approach, he/she is brilliantly sending the message back to the manager that this feedback is well received, appreciated, and beneficial to the employee's long-term success. (Try an active listening approach the next time you visit with your professor or manager!)

ETHICAL

Courtney has been a top performing real estate agent for the past five years straight. This success has brought positive publicity to her business, and several large developers and builders have approached her regarding future developments in the city. Last week Courtney took an impromptu phone call from a builder, and he is planning to build thirty-five houses next year. The average house will sell for approximately $300,000. He will need the help of a skilled realtor to get these homes sold!

On the call the builder stressed that he has already hired and fired three realtors in the past five years, and it seems apparent that realtors "don't get it!" Courtney asked him to elaborate on this concern, but all he would say is, "Every time I tell them what it is I want or need, they go ahead and do things differently! I want someone who wants to make a lot of money, but someone who understands my business concerns and pays attention to the details. If they would listen to me, things would go a lot smoother and I would have another twenty-five to forty houses for them to sell next year." Courtney made a mental note of that and scheduled a breakfast meeting at a local IHOP the following Tuesday at 9 a.m.

©SpeedKingz/Shutterstock.com

Tuesday morning came, and Courtney was on her way to meet the builder. At 8:50 a.m. she was pulling into the parking lot and suddenly realized that she forgot her briefcase. The briefcase contained her notepad, pens, business cards, and marketing materials. To make matters worse, she received a text message from the builder that he has already arrived at the restaurant and is excited to go over "many details" of their potential partnership.

What should Courtney do?

1. Call the builder and say she needs to run back to the office to get her briefcase, and therefore will be fifteen minutes late?

2. Attend to the meeting on time, but without the briefcase. She has been in this job for many years and has an excellent memory. Whatever they discuss, she will remember.

3. If none of the above, what specifically do you recommend Courtney do in this moment?

In the age of e-mails, text messages, calendar reminders, social media, push notifications, or even a long day at work, it is not uncommon to have a conversation with someone who is staring at their cell phone or television while you talk. This is commonly referred to as **distracted listening**.

Effective listening skills take practice and discipline. It starts with an awareness of the consequences of listening versus not listening. The more you are aware of the effects listening has on relationships, the more you are inclined to improve listening as a skill.

> ### *Distracted Listening*
> a person who is attempting to listen with their ears, but distracted with their eyes, mind, or body.

FIVE WAYS TO IMPROVE LISTENING SKILLS

1. Remove distractions.

This is a discipline anyone can administer, and is the best start to developing effective listening skills. Whether you are in management, professional sales, in the classroom with a professor, or simply having a conversation with your spouse, you can send a powerful signal by removing all distractions. Some notable distractions can be computers, cell phones, watches, food, push notifications, and more. Let's consider two scenarios in which removing distractions provides the listener with the moral high ground:

SCENARIO 1: Your girlfriend comes home from her server shift at the restaurant. It was a crazy and wild day, and she is considering quitting because her manager is too demanding. You listen to her every word, but your natural style of listening is to listen with the ears while looking straight at the television. On the bottom of the television screen you cannot help but notice the score of your favorite baseball team. They got blown out 10–0. Not meaning any harm, you bow your head and softly whisper "Oh come on!" Even though you are still listening with your ears, the body language and whisper may potentially be interpreted by the girlfriend as "he doesn't care."

SCENARIO 2: Your girlfriend comes home from her server shift at the restaurant. It was a crazy and wild day, and she is considering quitting because her manager is too demanding. You can see she is visibly upset and immediately shut the television off and walk over to her and say, "What happened today. Tell me all about it." The fact that you shut off the television and removed it as a distraction sends a powerful message that you are more concerned with her day than the television. You are now positioned to hear every word she says and provide thoughtful comments.

> Discuss amongst the class some of the negative impacts that students have experienced (business or personal) as a result of distracted listening.

2. Preparation is a requisite listening behavior, especially in the business community.

For example, if a client takes the time to confide all of their business needs with you, and you fail to take any notes it can inadvertently send the message that you are not detail oriented and do not care. As a rule of thumb, a business professional should always have a professional pad and paper to take notes and hold business cards. As your career evolves and the scope of projects become larger, professionals who take diligent notes are much better positioned to address the key concerns of the customer in the proposals. Here is an example of how removing distractions and preparation can demonstrate to a customer that you are truly listening:

Five to ten minutes prior to a conference call or meeting with a customer, suggested preparations:

- ✓ Clear distractions: e-mails, cell phone, including ringer—shut it off.

- ✓ Note pad ready: Write date, time, and names of people we are talking to. *Pronounce names correctly

- ✓ Know the agenda, purpose, and allotted time of meeting (respect their time)

  - • Listen. It's okay to say "I am here today to do some listening, and I have a few questions."

  - • When you are done listening—repeat back what you heard

- ✓ Have a drink of water—why water? H_2O hydrates and is oxygen for the brain.

- ✓ Close your eyes, be quiet for one minute, think about the outcome you expect, and breathe.

- ✓ Dial in five minutes early—do not be late. If they are late, tell them "No problem, I have the hour blocked out anyway."

3. Conversations or meetings can sometimes lose focus and therefore end poorly.

By **continuously evaluating** your audience (one person or many) you will be able to gauge the conversation and ensure the other party knows you are listening and maintain their best interest. For example, if you are speaking and can sense that the quietness is becoming noticeable, perhaps pause to ask if they are following you. Sometimes silence in a conversation is the innocuous result of them taking notes or processing what you are saying. Sometimes silence is a signal to the trained professional that he/she is talking too much or needs to slow down. In a conversation—especially high-level business conversations—continuously evaluating can be a brilliant tactic to deploy in order to ensure the customer's needs are being met.

4. Concentrating may be the simplest—yet, one of the most difficult—listening skills to master.

Efforts to concentrate can be greatly improved by removing distractions, preparation, and continuously evaluating. Statistics show that people can speak between 125 and 175 words a minute, but a person can listen at a rate of approximately 450 words per minute (Carver, Johnson, and Friedman 1970). A lot of information is flowing, and it's your job as an effective listener to concentrate, identify the important factors when someone speaks, and when the time is right repeat back what you heard. One of the most effective methods of practicing concentration skills is to **allow the other person to finish speaking before you begin speaking**. Finishing another person's sentence or interrupting a person before they finish speaking sends the message that you are not truly listening, but rather have already been preparing your own thoughts and response.

The three take-aways of concentration:

1. Listen to the other person's every word without interrupting

2. Repeat back what you heard; ask if you heard correctly

3. Ask if you can then address each concern

These three steps of concentration are even more powerful when a conversation (business or personal) is heated or cantankerous. If you deploy this method you can potentially reduce the temperature of the argument dramatically and swiftly!

5. Probing and asking the customer intelligent and insightful questions are another way to demonstrate and sharpen effective listening skills.

There are four recommended methods of asking sound, probing questions, designed to demonstrate that you are listening to the customer and can ultimately close the deal:

A. **O**pen Questions

B. **D**irective Questions

C. **R**eflective Questions

D. **E**arning Commitment

    ✓ "ODRE" (pronounced Ohh Dree)

Open questions are the beginning stage of probing questions. In this early stage of the questioning process it is recommended to ask questions that "open up" situations. For example, a realtor may start by asking "In a perfect world, what are the five most desirable things you want in buying a new home?" Asking such a broad, long-term, probing question will undoubtedly flush out that the customers want five bedrooms, location near an elementary school, cost under $350,000 (or meets their budget), has a three-car garage, and no association fees.

Directive questions, designed to garner clarity, should immediately follow open questions. For example, once the customer lists the top five preferences in a new home, the realtor is positioned to probe deeper and ask "Can you tell me a little more about why you prefer three garages?" Asking a direct question at this stage of the process may yield that the customers only have two cars but would like a third garage for their tools, lawn mower, and bicycles. (A house with two garages and a shed in the backyard for their lawnmower, may be possibly cheaper and more practical for their needs.)

Asking reflective questions positions the realtor to identify personal impacts to the customer, and ultimately offer solutions to mitigate those impacts. For example, the realtor may ask "Okay, so I understand your five most important aspects of a home. You provided me insight into each of those five important aspects. Now can you tell me about how a five-bedroom house near a school personally impacts you and your husband?" By asking reflective questions the realtor may decipher that attending their children's school functions and volunteering are strong family values and traditions that are important to their young family.

©Jacob Lund/Shutterstock.com

If you have performed the first three probing questions well, earning a commitment and asking for their business is a natural and appropriate final step in the process. For example, the realtor can say: "Okay, you provided me the five most important items you want in a new home. It sounds like you will accept a double garage as opposed to a triple garage if there is an acceptable shed in the backyard. Being next to an elementary school will allow you and your husband to more actively participate in school functions and take part in your children's education experience. If I can find you a house that meets these five major needs, within budget, and by an elementary school would you strongly consider making an offer on that home?"

By asking **probing questions** and following the ODRE process customers will be far more likely to feel you are genuinely listening to them and offering solutions to meet their specific business or personal needs.

CHAPTER SUMMARY

Most people tend to believe they are good listeners despite overwhelming research to dispute such claims. In an age of e-mails, texting, social media, radio, television, and cell phones, listening is becoming increasingly difficult. With all of these technological advances, distracted listening can easily infiltrate our lives and negatively impact our business and personal relationships. An argument can be made that with the advancement of globalization and significance of world politics, effective listening—as a skill—is now more important than ever before in human history. It's not enough to listen with just your ears. Effective listening includes listening with the ears, eyes, mind, and body.

For many, this requires a high level degree of concentration and discipline. Active listening occurs when the receiver in a conversation deliberately applies methods of verbal and/or non-verbal tactics in an effort to optimize the reception, interpretation, evaluation, and response to the one who is talking. Such tactics could be as simple as nodding your head in agreement when someone speaks, repeating back what you heard them say, demonstrating compassion for the speaker, and so on.

There are five recommended ways to help you immediately improve your listening skills: remove distractions, prepare for a conversation, continuously evaluate during a conversation, concentrate, and ask probing questions. In this chapter we showed you specifically how to approach a client with sharp listening skills and probing questions. The ODRE process—Open, Directive, Reflective, and Earning Commitment—is something you can start using today! If you interview for a job and the hiring manager asks how you approach new clients, consider telling them you use the ODRE

Probing Questions

a listening tactic that calls for asking open, directive, and reflective questions designed to meet the specific needs of a customer.

process! It demonstrates that you have useful skills on day 1 that will differentiate you from other candidates.

Professional sales coach and trainer Mark David says, "You need to slow it down to get ahead." In a society of immediacy "slowing it down" is almost an oxymoron. How can you slow things down and still get everything done? In your business and personal lives listening—truly listening—will enable you to slow things down and absorb the moment. Building a personal relationship with your spouse over thirty, forty, sixty years will require tremendous listening skills. The customers who tend to stay with you for a lifetime are the customers who feel you understand their needs and provide solutions to meet those needs.

REFERENCES

American Management Association. http://www.amanet.org/news/10076.aspx

Carver, Ronald P., Johnson, Raymond L., and Friedman, Herbert L. 1970. Factor analysis of the ability to comprehend time-compressed speech. Final report for the National Institute for Health. Washington, DC: American Institute for Research.

Nichols, Ralph G. and Stevens, Leonard A. 1957. "Listening to people." *Harvard Business Review* (Sept.). https://hbr.org/1957/09/listening-to-people

Steil, Lyman K., Barker, Larry L., and Watson, Kittie W. 1983. *Effective listening: Key to your business.* Addison-Wesley United States.

2 HOMEWORK

Anna Dietrich finished filling out her home mortgage application. While most people would be happy getting the home loan process going, Anna sighed, rolled her eyes, pushed the loan application toward the loan officer, and thought to herself "Here we go again." The bank's loan officer, Jamey Santengelo, could sense some consternation in Anna's face and commented, "You don't seem happy. You're buying a new house. These are exciting times. Is everything okay?"

Anna took a deep breath and said, "I have been through the home loan process before. And each time it seems like the loan officer calls with surprises or underwriting issues that cause the loan to be delayed. The last time I bought a house we had to reschedule the closing twice, and I had to rent a hotel because I had no place to stay. It seems like the loan officer and the underwriter fail to communicate, and it always affects me. So I am not looking forward to this process again."

Jamey nodded and said he understood. He promised that this experience would be different, and that he would communicate with the underwriter and Anna to ensure a smooth process. Anna grinned and said "Okay. Tell me how?"

QUESTION 1: If Jamey is truly listening to his client's concerns, what specific recommendations would you have for his response to Anna?

QUESTION 2: If Jamey originates and manages approximately fifteen to twenty loans per month, what recommendations do you have for him to deliver the same quality of service for every client?

CHAPTER 3
Sales Etiquette

You had me at hello.

— *Jerry Maguire,* movie, 1996

©michaeljungShutterstock.com

CHAPTER OBJECTIVES

✓ To develop a deeper understanding for the meaning and purpose of basic sales etiquette

✓ To discuss how sales etiquette can greatly impact your ability to attract and retain clients

✓ To demonstrate how the behaviors of sales etiquette can positively impact your personal relationships

✓ To explore five new ways to immediately improve your business etiquette

SALES ETIQUETTE

Cary and John are two hiring managers for KMB Pharmaceutical. After a grueling process of interviewing for a new sales representative in their southwest division, they have narrowed down their search to two impressive candidates. The regional manager has requested that a final decision be made by the close of business today. So Cary and John have decided to sit in the conference room and figure out which candidate would be the better fit for KMB.

It is not an easy decision because candidates A and B are almost a virtual tie; both have excellent professional selling experience that would easily qualify them for the job. Candidate A has fifteen years of professional sales experience in the industry and comes highly recommended from another internal sales representative. Candidate B has eleven years of professional selling experience, but has notably caught the eye of Cary and John having placed in the top 10 for sales volume during five of the last seven years. Put simply, candidate A has slightly more experience and comes recommended from an internal employee. Cary and John see value in employee referrals. Candidate B has slightly less experience, applied for the position through a recruiter, but is a top performer at his current company. Cary and John see the value in a candidate who is a consistent top performer. These are tough decisions to make for any hiring manager.

Suddenly the office manager enters the conference room holding two letters. She hands one to Cary and another to John. It appears candidate B swung by the lobby this morning and dropped off personal

thank you notes to Cary and John. The letters were short and concise, but spoke volumes. Cary began to read his letter out loud:

> Dear Cary, I just wanted to take a moment to thank you for the time and consideration you have afforded me during this interview process at KMB Pharmaceutical. These are truly exciting times at KMB as it appears the company's client base is expanding and revenues are increasing. I would like to reiterate my interest in joining the KMB team. My professional sales experience and ability to develop and maintain strategic relationships are attributes that could potentially add value to KMB and its shareholders. If you have any further questions or concerns that would assist in the decision-making process, please do not hesitate to reach out to me. I am excited to visit with you again soon. Thank you!

Two things immediately occurred to Cary and John: (1) candidate A had more experience and was recommended from within the company, but never did send a thank you note. And, (2) candidate B took the time to follow up with the decision makers and to thank each of them for their time. This very simple sales etiquette of saying thank you had transcending significance to Cary and John because this behavior would also be well received by the clients and would reflect positively on the KMB brand and its proud employees. It was one more added layer of comfort when making the final decision. In fact, John suggested that it is small attention to the details—like a thank you note—that have likely contributed to this candidate's top performance recognitions over the years. Cary and John finished their discussions and decided to select candidate B.

Relationships are won and lost on sales etiquette all the time, particularly in the early stages of a relationship when people are just getting acquainted with one another. How you dress for an interview is not only a reflection of your decency and sense of urgency, but your ability to adapt to the audience and appear appropriate. For example, a swanky tech company who prides itself on jeans and comfortable attire may find it odd if a candidate showed up at a job interview in a three-piece suit. While the candidate clearly took the time to look nice, dressing in a three-piece suit may appear inappropriate.

Sales Etiquette

standard and appropriate behaviors that align with a particular business setting, society, group, or class for the purpose of networking and relationship building.

In this chapter we will discuss the meaning of **sales etiquette**, engage in various sales etiquette techniques, and offer solutions to overcoming sales etiquette shortfalls.

FIVE WAYS TO IMPROVE YOUR SALES ETIQUETTE

1. Be Clear and Concise

Have a clear and concise message. One of the most famous lines in the 1996 hit movie *Jerry Maguire* was "Shut up. You had me at hello." In this scene Jerry Maguire (played by Tom Cruise) interrupts Dorothy Boyd (played by Renee Zellweger) to make a long-winded sales pitch of how much he loves her and needs her in his small company. Dorothy cuts him off mid-sentence and tells him that his lengthy sales pitch is unnecessary. You may recall in Chapter 2 we discussed how one of the most common mistakes professional sales representatives make on a regular basis is that they talk too much. It is not uncommon for a professional sales representative to leave a rambling four-minute voicemail with the goal of simply setting up a lunch with a client or saying thank you for their business.

Whether you are interviewing for a job, engaging a client, or texting a business acquaintance, you are in the business of selling. As sales professionals we have a lot to say, but we fail to realize that our customers are busy and probably have many other voicemails, e-mails, text messages, and meetings to attend. A lengthy, rambling voicemail to a new customer can be potentially perceived as inappropriate, rude, or . . . weird. For purposes of "having a clear message" the proper etiquette is to begin your voicemail, e-mail, text, letter,with a pleasantry, then pivot to the purpose for calling or writing, and then always finish with "Thank you." For example, "Hello Bob, it's Sheila Smith from the bank. I hope you are having a terrific day. I just wanted to inform you that your loan documents are prepared and ready for you to review. Please feel free to pick them up at the bank any time this week. Thank you." This message was clear, concise, substantive, and only took approximately fifteen seconds to say and less than ten seconds to read.

We spend the majority of our college career learning to write lengthy and well thought out term papers and essays. But rarely do we see courses that focus on concise and pithy messaging. In fact, many of you taking this course will soon find yourselves writing cover letters to prospective employers seeking to hire you. In other words, your resume and cover letters are considered a very important part of your sales pitch to the respective employer. Therefore proper etiquette and professionalism may be the differentiator between you and the other candidates. Let's take a closer look at etiquette for cover letters. We will look at a sample cover letter shortly, but the secret to a cover letter—and how they differ from resumes—is that it puts the needs of the company first, and then articulates how YOUR background, skills, education, and experience will meet those needs. However, research indicates that hiring managers do not want to read a rambling, lengthy cover letter. According to a 2011 Orange County Survey, 70 percent of employers prefer a cover letter to be 250 words or less! (Hilden 2011) In other words you have about half a page—or less—to make your pitch!

TIPS TO WRITING OR SPEAKING CONCISE STATEMENTS

✓ Writing: Begin e-mails, text messages, or cover letters with kind words: "Hi Sarah, I hope your weekend was terrific." Or "Hi Sarah, thank you so much for the note. I'm happy to . . ."

✓ Calling: Keep voicemails to forty-five words or fifteen seconds: your name, purpose of the call, define the call to action, always say thank you. This does not mean rush the call, but rather keep it substantive.

✓ Selling: Do not TELL the customer what they need or what they should do. Instead, make a suggestion(s) or a recommendation(s).

✓ Heated customer, spouse, parent, or coworker: If they are angry with you, start by acknowledging their concern and let them know you appreciate them bringing this to your attention. Beginning the message in this manner dramatically reduces the temperature of the aggravated party.

04/04/2018

Ms. Becky Dietrich
Human Resources Manager
ABC Pharm Company, Inc.
145 Beach 112th Street
Myrtle Beach, South Carolina 29272

RE: Pharmaceutical Sales Representative

Dear Ms. Dietrich:

I am writing you in regard to the Pharmaceutical Sales Position currently posted on your website. The position requires 3–5 years professional sales experience, preferably in healthcare. My background consists of 7 years in professional sales with the previous 2 years serving in the capacity of medical sales representative for Denver-based Strike Company. In that capacity I worked directly with the Physicians and Procurement Managers from local hospitals who were in the market to upgrade Ultrasound machines.

Additionally, my education as a Registered Nurse (RN) may be of further interest to you as ABC Pharm Company seeks candidates who have a desirable blend of sales and healthcare credentials. I have also included my resume for your consideration and review, and you will notice that I have considerable networking experience having been tasked with managing each of Strike Company's last 4 healthcare conferences in Denver.

If you believe my professional experience, education, and networking capabilities with healthcare professionals are a match for your current business needs, I would appreciate an opportunity to meet with you and further discuss the Pharmaceutical Sales Position. Thank you kindly.

Sincerely,

Paul Aughinbaugh, R.N.

2. *Recommend or Suggest*

Sales professionals make recommendations and suggestions. They do not tell clients what to do. A common mistake that plagues consultants in marketing, business development, and sales is that they tell the client what to do. For example, consider the situation in which a marketing director of a construction company is making recommendations to the senior management team. The company has been around for forty years and operates throughout the Southwest United States.

SCENARIO 1: Marketing Director: "We need to start spending more time networking with the City of Albuquerque. Next month they are going to pass a bond that will create tens of millions in new construction, and if we don't act right now we are going to miss this opportunity and have a painful year watching our competition get ahead."

SCENARIO 2: Marketing Director: "The City of Albuquerque is poised to pass a bond next month that will approve tens of millions of dollars in new construction. I would like to make a recommendation to the senior management team that we consider dedicating some resources to networking with city officials, and positioning ourselves to capture some of these opportunities."

In scenario 1, the marketing director has good intentions and is pointing out some useful information to the senior management team. But his choice of words is painting a grim picture; that is, we either act on this right now—or else! Members of the senior management team may perceive their marketing director as slightly pompous and assuming. After all, the company has survived for forty years, and many of the senior managers have been around for a long time, finding success in a variety of ways. In scenario 2, the marketing director has identified a unique business opportunity and is choosing his words carefully, asking the senior management team to "consider" putting some of the company's resources behind this idea. Furthermore, the marketing director has now set the stage for senior managers to weigh in on how THEY see the Albuquerque opportunity without the sense of doom and gloom presented in scenario 1. When applied correctly, this basic sales etiquette of "recommending" and "suggesting" to a customer or a colleague could have a tremendous impact on your ability to move a discussion forward or closing the deal.

3. *Proper Amount of Eye Contact*

Generally speaking people make eye contact about 30–60 percent of the time (Cornell Research 2014). Too little eye contact can imply untrustworthiness, nervousness, or that you do not care. Too much eye contact can

©fizkes/Shutterstock.com

cause the buyer to become uncomfortable, signifying that you are angry, arrogant, or attempting to dominate. Therefore, knowing the proper balance of eye contact can provide you a competitive advantage in professional selling. It is also one of the most basic forms of sales etiquette that is easy to practice but never to be underestimated. According to *Forbes* editorial contributor, Carol Goman, too much eye contact can give the buyer the impression that you are condescending or rude (Goman 2014).

In a small audience of two people or less (for example a married couple sitting at your desk), the proper amount of eye contact while speaking should be no more than seven to ten seconds for each person. After approximately ten seconds, shift your eye contact to the other person in the conversation. For a larger audience you will have more people in the room to address. Therefore, it is recommended that you spend an average of no more than three to five seconds looking at one person (Ben Decker, chief executive officer of Decker Communications in San Francisco). Consider practicing proper eye contact when you are storytelling with your friends or talking to your parents.

4. Be Complimentary

As sales professionals we undoubtedly have competitors who seek the same clients we do. Sales professionals are naturally competitive people. We instinctively want to win. There is no worse feeling than losing a customer to a competitor, and there is no better feeling than winning a new client from the competition. In a professional selling career, you will experience both! Additionally, customers may like working with YOU, but do not like your organization, its strict rules, the regulations, fees, or many other factors. As a rule of thumb, do not engage in disparaging your competitors, boss, colleagues, vendors, former customers, or anybody.

Consider the two scenarios below:

SCENARIO 1: Jim has been a customer at your bank for ten years. One day he begins to give you a compliment that you are the best banker he has ever had, but he is frustrated that your bank has a policy of charging $25 for a "bounced check." Empathizing with the customer, the banker listens to Jim's point of view but politely explains that "Every bank has this policy— and for good reasons: (1) Jim, despite having insufficient funds in your account, we have always stood by you and ensured the person receiving your check got paid. We do that because we value your relationship. But Jim we have thousands of customers and there are times customers do not pay us back for honoring the check. The $25 fee helps offset the occasional losses and risks associated with check bouncing. And, (2) the fees serve as a deterrent to customers who do not adequately manage their account."

Hearing the reasoning and professional explanation of the banker, Jim nods and says he understands and needs to do a better job managing his checking account.

SCENARIO 2: Jim has been a customer at your bank for ten years. One day he begins to give you a compliment that you are the best banker he has ever had, but he is frustrated that your bank has a policy of charging $25 for a "bounced check." The banker does not like the awkward situation and

©fizkes/Shutterstock.com

responds, "Ya, Jim I agree. Banks can be greedy. Our bank president has a huge home and a corner office, but yet our good customers like you have to pay excessive penalties for making a simple mistake."

In scenario 1, the banker empathized with the customer and remained complimentary. Yet he remained professional and walked Jim through the reasoning for such fees. Since Jim is aware every bank has this policy, he eventually admits that he needs to do a better job of managing his account. In scenario 2, the banker gives the impression that the financial institution is greedy. The banker should not be surprised if Jim moves his accounts to another bank someday. Be careful when such situations occur, because how you respond is a direct reflection of your personal character and professional sales etiquette. You may believe at the time that the customer is happy you agree with them in private, but in actuality you may lose the customer by gossiping and being negative.

Politics is another topic that could negatively impact your professional selling capabilities, particularly in the early stages of a relationship. The topic of politics will undoubtedly come up in professional selling conversations. And sometimes the client may push you hard to state which political candidate you favor the most, or what you think of a particular policy. When this situation occurs (and it will occur), we recommend that you simply remain positive and complimentary without engaging too deeply in this portion of the conversation. For example, if a presidential election is one month away and your customer begins to disparage one of the candidates, your best option is to be complimentary and say something like, "I hope whomever wins does a great job and makes us all proud." Be careful with politics in professional selling conversations. Even when you agree on a particular candidate, you may reference a certain innocuous policy that makes the client uncomfortable.

Underpromising and Overdelivering

setting upfront expectations with customers that are fair, appropriate, and aligned with company precedent while taking active steps to exceed these expectations in a manner that does not comprise the quality of the product/service.

5. Underpromise, but Overdeliver

One of the most common mistakes in professional selling is overpromising and underdelivering. Most of the time these promises are made with the very best intentions, and yet it is one of the most avoidable mistakes. It is also a professional selling etiquette that you can deploy at the earliest stages of your sales career. It should be expected that customers, for example, will ask if delivery of their product/service can be expedited, or if the closing date can be "moved up," or if fees can be waived, or if your boss wants to have your project completed by Friday, and so forth. Naturally, in an effort to get the customer to sign the contract at that moment (or the boss to like you), professional sales representatives will make promises for outcomes they have minimal control over.

One way to manage expectations with external customers is to identify the timeline and expectations of your interdepartmental support team. In a bank, the loan officer may originate loans, but the loan processors, underwriters, and other team members may have a thirty-day closing policy. If the customer would like their loan to close quicker than thirty days, do not agree to an expedited closing without first receiving direct input from all internal support team members. It is recommended to tell the customer upfront that loan closings take an average of thirty days; however, you will visit with both the processor and underwriter first thing tomorrow and get their input about an expedited closing. Tell the customer you will call them within forty-eight hours to see what options the bank has come up with!

ETHICAL

Mark Johnson is the business development manager for a national full service engineering company. His primary responsibility is to build inroads and develop relationships with businesses and municipalities who have a need for engineering services. He has been making marketing calls to Brick Construction Company for more than a year when suddenly an e-mail pops up from Kelly Dietrich, "Hi Mr. Johnson, this is Kelly Dietrich from Brick Construction Company. I am calling on behalf of the Director of Construction, Toni D'Amico. Toni has received your marketing materials and appreciates you reaching out. Do you have time to meet myself and Toni tomorrow for lunch to discuss your engineering services and to learn a little more about Brick Company? There is a great burger restaurant down the street from our office, and if your schedule permits we could meet you at 12 p.m."

Smiling ear to ear that his marketing efforts are finally paying off, he replies, "Hi Kelly! Tomorrow at 12 p.m. works perfect, and if it is okay with you I would like to bring our Civil Engineer Manager, Bob Thompson, in case you have more technical questions. Looking forward to the meeting!"

The following day Mark and Bob arrive at the restaurant and immediately begin scanning the tables to see if two men are sitting waiting. All of the tables appear to be filled with families or couples having lunch, so they begin to think they have arrived before Toni and Kelly. They decide to inform the host that they will need a table for four adults, but that they are still awaiting two more gentlemen named Toni and Kelly. The host nods and says he will keep an eye out for them. Suddenly, two women standing just a couple feet away—dressed in professional attire—approach Mark and say, "Mark Johnson? Hi, I am Kelly Dietrich, and this is our Director of Construction, Toni D'Amico." Mark was shocked and noticeably embarrassed. He thought Toni and Kelly would be men, as most of his construction clients seem to be men. He had just referred to his potential customers as "gentlemen," and he is 100 percent certain Kelly and Toni overheard his comments.

What should Mark do?

1. Act like nothing happened and move on with the pleasantries? Maybe they didn't overhear anything.

2. Apologize? Admit you made a mistake and address the fact that they may be offended.

3. Is there another way to handle this awkward situation?

4. What proactive steps could Mark and Bob take the next time to avoid such an embarrassing first meeting? Do you have any advice for how Mark and Bob should treat these professional women when they sit down and have the lunch?

CHAPTER SUMMARY

In this chapter we discussed a variety of ways in which sales etiquette could be the differentiator in your approach to business. As we have seen with the KMB Pharmaceutical story at the beginning of the chapter, a simple thank you note was the difference in one candidate earning the job over the other candidate.

People are busy and they have a lot going on in their personal and business lives. Having a clear and concise message is one way for you to ensure that customers do not get confused or frustrated. For example, leaving a four-minute voicemail can potentially frustrate a customer. If you cannot deliver a message in twenty to thirty seconds it may be best not leaving a voicemail at all. We also talked about how too many sales professionals "tell" the customers what is best for them, or what they should do. A true professional makes a recommendation, suggestion, or offers advice. Try practicing making "recommendations" and you will notice quickly that customers appreciate your approach.

Remember that eye contact is a very important sales etiquette behavior. We discussed small and large audiences, and if done correctly you will balance the room well. If done poorly you run the risk of offending a guest or coming across as untrustworthy.

Another way to demonstrate good character and superior sales etiquette is to avoid engaging in negative conversations about people or companies. Remember, people want to be associated with winners. Talking negative about others can sometimes backfire and be perceived by customers that you are unethical. Be complimentary about others and focus the conversation on the many positives you bring to the customer.

Lastly, one of the mistakes many sales professionals make is that we promise too much and then fail to adequately honor those promises. If you promised documents by Thursday, it's not acceptable to deliver them by Friday afternoon. Sales professionals naturally want to be everything to everybody. It's a flawed philosophy to overpromise, and you may be setting yourself up for failure. True professionals set adequate and appropriate expectations with their customers—based off precedent. The same proves true in your personal lives. If you tell your significant other that you will arrive at 6 p.m., then you should be there no later than 6 p.m. Sounds simple, but people who often arrive late find themselves branded "always late" and this negatively impacts their credibility when making promises.

You now have five ways that you can begin to enhance and improve your professional selling etiquette.

REFERENCES

Cornell Research. https://www.forbes.com/sites/carolkinseygoman/2014/08/21/facinating-facts-about-eye-contact/#210030f61e26

Decker, Ben. https://www.wsj.com/articles/SB10001424127887324809804578511290822228174

Goman, Carol K. 2014. "Fascinating Facts about Eye Contact." *Forbes* (August 21). http://www.forbes.com/sites/carolkinseygoman/2014/08/21/facinating-facts-about-eye-contact/#63c52f97518b)

Hilden, Eric. 2011. The 2011 Orange County Resume Survey. Saddleback College, Mission Viejo, CA. http://www.saddleback.edu/uploads/jobs/documents/The2011OrangeCountyResumeSurvey.pdf

3 HOMEWORK

As the business development and sales manager for his engineering company, it was Lonnie's job to set face-to-face meetings with his civil engineering team and local developers from the community. Local developers are known for developing commercial and residential property, and the projects almost always require civil engineers to help with the upfront design and due diligence. Lonnie received a phone call from a local developer asking if Lonnie's civil engineering team had time for lunch today to discuss a potential project. "Absolutely," Lonnie replied. "I'll gather the team and we will meet you at Billy's Burgers at 12 p.m."

A bit later, both entities were seated at Billy's Burgers. The meeting started out cordial, and everyone placed their lunch orders. As soon as the waiter took the meal order and walked away, one of the developers said, "This President Obama is going to run this country through the floor. With all of his regulations and government policies it's a miracle we can get anything done anymore. Lonnie, what does your company think about President Obama? And what about you guys (engineers)? Do you guys agree or disagree with us?"

Lonnie and his two engineering colleagues were put on the spot, but after two to three seconds of silence it became apparent that someone from Lonnie's team needed to speak up!

QUESTION 1: What advice do you have for Lonnie and his engineering colleagues?

QUESTION 2: If a client wants to speak about reasonable public policy, does the sales representative have an obligation to take the higher road and listen with an open mind?

Part Two

Targeting Your Audience and Positioning

CHAPTER 4
Networking and Prospecting

Even if you're on the right track, you can still get run over if you're moving too slowly.

— *Roy Rogers*

©Rawpixel.com/Shutterstock.com

CHAPTER OBJECTIVES

✓ Develop an understanding and appreciation for networking

✓ Discuss how networking or prospecting can impact your personal life

✓ Discover five ways to network or prospect

✓ Methods for managing and following up with your network and prospects (CRM systems, social networking)

✓ Discuss how referrals can help launch your professional selling career

Senior Vice President of Sales, Chuck Schumacher, received an e-mail about a conference coming up in Scottsdale, Arizona. He was just about to delete the e-mail when something caught his eye. It appeared that two of the main sponsors of the conference were also two of his company's top ten clients. If his top clients were attending the conference, maybe this merited a closer look.

As Chuck became more curious about this conference he also noticed there was a link with an attendee list of business professionals already signed up for the conference. Chuck began to review the list, and as he read through many of the attendees he recalled that some of these names were discussed at his last sales meeting between him and his regional sales staff.

Deciding to pursue this conference further he summoned his sales manager, Kathy Smith, to his office.

Chuck: "Hi Kathy, and thanks for coming right over."

Kathy, "My pleasure. What can I do for you Chuck?"

Chuck: "Well, I received an e-mail about a conference coming up in Scottsdale, and two of our top clients are sponsors at this event. If I remember correctly from our last sales meeting, we have not spent any face time with these two clients in the past four to five months. Maybe this conference is a good way to run into them and get some

©Monkey Business Images/Shutterstock.com

face time. Also, as I review the attendee list, some of the other attendees seem to ring a bell. For example, at our sales meeting on Monday you and Martha mentioned that State Bank would be an ideal account for our company, and that you have been trying to get ahold of their head of procurement, Mark, for six months now with no luck. Is that correct?"

Kathy: "That is correct. He is a potential client that would fit our business strategy perfectly, but I have not seen him at any of the local social networking events, and the one time I left a voicemail he never called me back. I would jump at the opportunity to meet him and talk about our services."

Chuck: "Well, he's attending this conference in Scottsdale, and I wonder if you could call him again and see if there was an opportunity to meet for breakfast, lunch, coffee, or whatever. The conference is not very expensive, and we know he will be there for sure. You've been talking about this account for six months."

Upon leaving Chuck's office, Kathy made a call over to Mark at State Bank and he confirmed that he *would* be attending the conference. He also expressed that he would definitely appreciate an opportunity to meet Kathy and grab coffee or lunch. The two exchanged cell phone numbers, and Kathy made it a promise that she would attend the conference and give him a call to connect up.

NETWORKING AND PROSPECTING

When the authors of this textbook were developing this chapter on networking and prospecting, we recalled a sales manager's famous weekly reminder, "Keep your pipeline full, and have more people to see than you have time to see." This advice of keeping a pipeline full of prospects is universally true because a business always runs the risk of losing a customer. Even if a business successfully retains 92 percent of its client base—which is outstanding—they are still losing 8 percent of their customers in any given year. Sometimes these customers are large accounts with significant revenue implications. Networking and prospecting are the antidote to Roy Rogers' famous quote at the beginning of this chapter.

Are networking and prospecting the same? Technically not quite, but in the effort to maintain a steady pipeline of new customers and leads they are inextricable to a professional sales representative.

Therefore, **networking** is defined as the cultivation of productive relationships for personal, employment, or business purposes. **Prospecting** is defined as the art of developing a new or previous relationship with a purpose of converting to new business over time. The difference between the two is that while networking focuses on productive relationships—such as forming a relationship with city council members—these relationships may or may not become customers; whereas, prospecting focuses on relationships who you specifically would like to become customers in due time.

For example, a land developer usually needs the support and approval of its local city or county officials before developing a parcel of land. If your company provided civil engineering services for developers, you may "network" and build relationships with city officials because those relationships may prove valuable for your developer customers; however, the developer would be your prospect, not the city officials. The developer may have three civil engineer firms to choose from, but will likely choose your firm due to its inroads and relationships with city or county officials.

Another way to differentiate a prospect versus a network is to fully understand what QUALIFIES someone/business as a prospect. If you have a list of prospects, a sales manager should be able to ask three simple questions: (1) Does this person/business have a need for our product/or service; (2) are the person(s) you are marketing to in a decision-making capacity? And (3A) can the company afford your product/service, (3B) are the person(s) you are marketing to in a position to approve payment or get you paid? If a sales professional replies "no" to ANY one of these

Networking

the cultivation of productive relationships for personal, employment, or business purposes.

Prospecting

the art of developing a new or previous relationship with a purpose of converting to new business over time.

three questions, the authors take the position that you do not technically have a prospect. For example, let's assume a commercial banker meets a restaurant manager at the local Chamber of Commerce network event, and the restaurant manager tells the banker that his boss (restaurant owner) is considering expanding the patio and may need a bank loan in the near future. This is great news: a business with financial needs, and a manager who wants to keep in touch. In the bank's weekly sales meeting the sales manager may ask—or has the RIGHT to ask—about this "prospect" and the likelihood of a loan coming to fruition. The commercial banker would have to admit that while this is a warm lead he/she has NOT met the owner of this restaurant . . . just yet. Fact is, this restaurant manager is not the decision-maker, and not in a position to get the banker to start drafting paperwork. Therefore, the authors would conclude this restaurant manager is in your business "network" but does not qualify as a prospect. The restaurant manager is a productive relationship that can be of value in this process.

The point? By being able to CLEARLY distinguish between what your network is versus who your (qualified) prospects are can greatly impact a sales manager's ability to coach the banker and his/her future behaviors. For example, brainstorming ideas, drafting talking points, and/or deploying effective techniques to get in FRONT of the restaurant owner IS the new mission. Once the restaurant owner is at the table . . . we now have a prospect worthy of our added time and resources. Otherwise, every sales meeting will be the same report: "I'm still keeping in touch with the manager, Don Berg, and hopefully something will happen soon." While both networking and prospecting are necessary in business, knowing the fundamental difference between the two will help with efficiency and accountability.

TWO SUGGESTIONS TO FACTOR INTO NETWORKING AND PROSPECTING

1. Network or prospect with a purpose.

One way to prospect with a purpose is to focus on the kinds of customers you are most comfortable with. If you are a banker who provides commercial loans, and you are most comfortable with men and women from the construction industry, then it is recommended that you target the construction industry. If doctors and lawyers make you uncomfortable, then avoid that part of the industry. Find your niche, your comfort level, and go for it!

Note to Student

In your list of fifty, if several prospects seem to never materialize, consider removing them from the list and replacing them with several new leads. This way, you always have a fresh list of fifty prospects that you highly desire. In many industries there are hundreds of prospects. Maybe thousands! However, it is recommended to have your top fifty wish list derived from the company's master list.

2. *Make a wish list of customers or clients you would LIKE to network or prospect.*

List at least fifty names of people that you realistically have a chance to do business with, and make sure this list has a "top 5–10" names that are *most* desirable for your strategy. For example, you're a banker. And in your market there are five to seven construction companies who perfectly match your sales strategy: they each have less than forty employees, one decision-maker who is easy to access, and they operate in the same vicinity as your bank.

FIVE WAYS TO NETWORK OR PROSPECT

1. *Target* relevant *conferences that your customers attend.*

In any given industry there are many local, regional, national, and even international conferences to attend. It's foolish and even unrealistic to attend every conference. They can be expensive and many times poorly orchestrated. But you can sit down with your manager and articulate how your "list of fifty contacts" seems to be attending the same two conferences every year. In fact, conferences provide you with an excuse to contact your top 50. For example, "Hi Bob! I just wanted to see if you are attending any of the upcoming developer conferences coming up this quarter?" In your list of fifty, you may find that six are attending the same conference. Now you can see if these six have time for a hello, coffee, breakfast, lunch, dinner, and more. Another unintended consequence of attending relevant conferences is you naturally run into old friends, or neighbors you hardly speak with, or people in the community who are valuable to know (politicians, recruiters, business executives). These relationships will potentially open new doors that you never even considered.

2. *Network or prospect by joining* relevant *industry committees.*

Almost every industry has committees, task forces, governing bodies, board of directors (business and charity). For example, the railroad industry has AREMA as a means to network. AREMA hosts one large conference each year, and embodies many committees that meet regularly. The railroad industry—and all of its affiliated members—can join the committees and participate in the process. Another example is Valley Partnership in Phoenix, Arizona. Valley Partnership is the business network community open to ALL businesses in Phoenix. They meet every month for breakfast with a purpose of networking, prospecting, and keeping abreast of industry trends. Valley Partnership has several committees such as communications, transportation, golf, federal issues committee, and more. Most of these committees are open for members to join, and they meet once a month or quarter for about one hour. You will find that some of the people on these committees are the same people and businesses your company *wants* to do business with. It's an excellent way to get your name out there, build credibility, network, and prospect. Many times, some of the people you network with or prospect to may never become your customer—but—do not be surprised if a recruiter or hiring manager takes notice of how you strategically network and prospect. You may find yourself recruited or offered a new job!

3. Attend local city, county, state, and federal social events.

For example, the Arizona Department of Transportation (ADOT) may host a Christmas fundraiser for the poor. The local Chamber of Commerce— found in almost every municipality in America—hosts social networking and prospecting events. Many times local businesses and entities attend these social events, and it is a great way to network or "bump into" some of the targeted prospects you may have.

4. Host your own networking event!

If you are a banker, realtor, or construction company, perhaps suggest that your local facility offer an annual customer service appreciation event, or sponsor your own charity event. Most companies already have quarterly or annual networking events. But if you don't, perhaps make a suggestion about hosting one in the near future. This could be an excellent way to network with the community or to invite members from your prospect list. For example, a Realtor in Pinal County, Arizona, brings his former customers to an annual rodeo. This is a unique way to stay in front of your customers, show appreciation, and network for new leads.

Another way to host your own prospecting event is to offer free webinars or in-house training. If you are a banker, perhaps offer a webinar or in-house training for first-time homebuyer loans. You could even **partner** with a prospect—such as a local realtor who sends you business—to run the event. It's an excellent way to expand your network and get face time with prospects. Hosting your own events also helps enhance your credibility in the business community. If you are offering training or classes, you may be

©Peter WeberShutterstock.com

perceived as the home loan guru or "thought leader." As a result you may naturally receive unsolicited referrals!

Lastly, and perhaps the simplest way to network or prospect is to . . .

5. Be part of your neighborhood schools, little league baseball or girls' soccer.

Local schools need support from the business community, and they are almost always in need of volunteers. This is a great strategy to not only make a difference in the community, and be part of your local education process, but it is also a venue in which you will meet countless other parents, business leaders, and industry influentials (we will discuss influentials in greater detail in Chapter 5). As we authored this book, I recalled my early days in my banking career in which I had the good fortune of meeting my market president the first day on the job. I had two young daughters at the time, and the market president told me, "John, make sure you never miss any school or volunteer opportunities with your kids. You'll be a happier person if you do these things, and you will meet other business leaders from the community when you are there." She was 100 percent correct, and I can personally attest to the fact that many of my banking loans came from being part of the local community schools and sports institutions.

These are five excellent ways to not only network or prospect, but also a good way to convince a hiring manager that you have **several ideas** on day one how you could connect with people and grow your business.

Okay, let's assume you put these concepts into practice, and you begin strategically attending conferences or committee events. What do you say if a potential prospect at the committee meeting says to you: "I noticed you are a payroll software sales professional. I have been meaning to speak with you but I keep missing you at these meetings. My company has grown from a start-up with five people into eighty-five and growing. Payroll is becoming unmanageable for me, and it is impacting my employee morale and our customers are also taking notice. What can Whitney's Payroll software do for me?"

VALUE PROPOSITION

Many of us have heard the term "30-second elevator ride speech," sales pitch, or value proposition. For the purposes of networking and prospecting, we have decided to call this developing a **value proposition**. A value proposition is a brief statement used by sales professionals toward a person or business to express how the value of their services can make a specific

> *Value Proposition*
>
> a brief statement used by sales professionals toward a person or business to express how the value of their services can make a specific impact with realistic and measurable results.

impact with realistic and measurable results. Let's consider the situation above in which a prospect asks what value our services will do for their company. Here is a well scripted value proposition versus a poorly scripted value proposition:

Example of a Well Scripted Value Proposition

> "Whitney's Payroll Software Company can improve its customer retention rate by a minimum of 5 percent in a one-year period in its Dallas market by implementing our customer retention training for its professional sales personnel."

Example of a Poorly Scripted Value Proposition

> "If you sign up for our customer retention training program, you can expect that Whitney's Payroll Software Company will save you money."

Value Propositions are:

- ✓ Organized, prepared, and purposeful

- ✓ No more than twenty-five to thirty seconds in length (*remember that for every ninety words written down on paper equates to approximately thirty seconds of speaking)

- ✓ Specific and have trigger words: For example, 10 percent improvement in year #1, market share, client retention, customer satisfaction. States the facts based off your company precedent

- ✓ Focused mainly on "value" and potential impact to a prospect's company

CLASS EXERCISE (20–25 MINUTES)

Break students into groups of five to seven, and task them with choosing a business and developing a value proposition. After each group presents their value proposition students should be encouraged to provide constructive criticism about each group's value proposition.

ETHICAL DILEMMA

Armstrong Network, Inc. sent four members of its sales team to attend the 2018 I.T. Conference in Las Vegas. The goal was threefold: set up a marketing booth to showcase its services, network with others attending the conference, and meet Trader Company's Director of I.T., Bill Smith (a highly desired prospect that Armstrong Network, Inc. has been targeting for the past eight months). Each member of the Armstrong Network team was dressed professionally, wore proper name tags, and brought business cards to exchange with other professionals. Additionally, they each developed a value proposition, and now the time had come to meet people and expand their network.

After a couple of hours of talking to visitors at their booth, the Armstrong sales team seemed pleased with the interest in their booth and volume of potential new prospects. Suddenly, one of the members of the Armstrong sales team, Tom Connors, noticed that Trader Company's Director of I.T., Bill Smith—along with three of his colleagues—were walking straight past their booth! Tom came out from behind the booth with the intent of locking eyes with Mr. Smith and potentially wooing him over to the Armstrong booth to meet the team. Tom caught eyes with Mr. Smith and gestured for him to come over, but it appeared Mr. Smith had no intention of stopping by the Armstrong Network booth. Unfazed and undeterred to meet this prospect, Tom approached Mr. Smith and extended his hand and introduced himself. The two exchanged pleasantries and began making small talk.

©rkl_foto/Shutterstock.com

Within thirty seconds Tom realized that Mr. Smith was checking his cell phone and glancing ahead at other booths. Mr. Smith's body language clearly indicated his interest was minimal and he wanted to move on to check out other booths at the conference. Armstrong Network's sales manager, Kathy Beckett, was happy to see Tom making conversation with Mr. Smith, but quickly noticed that the prospect's body language indicated he would soon walk away from Tom. As the team's sales manager this gave Kathy concern because they have wanted to talk with Mr. Smith for eight months, and here was their golden opportunity. What should Kathy do?

A. Stay out of it. Tom is a professional and if Mr. Smith is not interested in talking, it will only become more uncomfortable if others from Armstrong join the conversation.

B. Go talk to Mr. Smith's colleagues with the hope that Mr. Smith will now have an excuse to keep talking to Tom.

C. Join the conversation with Tom and Mr. Smith before Mr. Smith heads off to the next booth. Since this is a highly desired prospect, it makes perfect sense for Kathy to introduce herself and express that the team was hoping to say hello.

Networking and Prospecting are absolutely necessary for a sales professional to keep a pipeline full of potential customers. However, a huge challenge for most sales professionals is that 44 percent give up after just one follow-up (Tousley 2017). Some research has concluded that 80 percent of earning a sale requires as many as five follow-ups after the initial contact (Tousley 2017). In other words, one of the key reasons that sales professionals fail to advance the business conversation with prospects is because they make the initial contact but do not adequately and appropriately follow up with the client. Keep this in mind as you launch a career in professional selling!

Customer Relationship Management (CRM) System

all the tools, technologies, and procedures to manage, improve, or facilitate sales, support, and related interactions with customers, prospects, and business partners throughout the enterprise.

One of your primary responsibilities in professional selling is to network and prospect, but it is next to impossible to remember the names of hundreds—or even thousands—of people that you have met during your professional career. A **Customer Relationship Management (CRM) system** is the best practice for managing your customer database. A CRM system is defined as: all of the tools, technologies, and procedures to manage, improve, or facilitate sales, support and related interactions with customers, prospects, and business partners throughout the enterprise (Sweeney Group). Most companies have advanced CRM systems such as SalesForce.com, Vision, or NetSuite. These CRM systems are technologically superior, efficient, and proven to drive a return on investment (ROI). However, such advanced systems can be expensive and are not always necessary (depending on the company size or targeted industry). There are basic tools such as Excel spreadsheets that can provide client management support.

Regardless of which CRM tool you deploy in your professional selling career, the take-away is that you enact the discipline of keeping and maintaining an accurate database of your prospects with the goal of keeping in touch and strengthening the relationships. As a tip, the authors of this textbook recommend ranking your prospects in an order of importance: for example, A's, B's, and C's (with the "A prospects" receiving your best efforts and most resources, and the "C prospects" receiving the least). CRM spreadsheets should provide you with these five basic functions:

- ✓ Business name, and the names of decision-makers

- ✓ Proper contact information for the decision-makers

- ✓ Accurate dates and notes of prior interactions. For example: What are the details from the last meeting? Is there a proposal opportunity coming up? Is there a budget? What are next steps? Details of what is important to the client: names of their family members, hobbies they shared with you, or any other important facts that will help develop the relationship and advance the conversation

- ✓ Tickler/reminders set up that remind you when to follow up with the customer (if they asked for a call in two weeks, then make sure you call in two weeks!)

- ✓ Level of importance: A = high probability of making a sale. C = low probability, but worth keeping in touch with the client

There are far more capabilities and functions in CRM systems, but for the purposes of this chapter we will focus on the basic needs and functions of customer relationship management.

Remember we began Chapter 1 with Trustworthiness and Relatability. If you are married, did you ask your spouse to marry you on the first date? Probably not. The relationship started with building trust and finding ways to relate to each other. The conversation kept evolving, and eventually you decided to tie the knot. Professional selling principles are not much different from personal relationships, and many times the principles discussed in this book can be used in your personal lives. Too often sales professionals make the mistake of beginning a business conversation with "Here's what my company does, and we would like to show you all of our products/services." The authors recommend beginning any conversation (business or personal) with basic rapport. For example, how are you; was hoping to meet you; my cousin went to college with you…. There are so many ways to begin a conversation and build basic trust and relatability. There will be *plenty* of time in a conversation to make your sales pitch.

Fear of networking and prospecting is nothing to take for granted. Some people have an easy time connecting with others, but most of us (even the very best sales professionals) can get nervous or fearful of meeting a new client or prospect. A healthy dose of fear can actually be useful if it helps you organize and prepare for meetings. However, fear is not good when it polarizes us, causing us to remain distant and quiet in a room full of 500 people. Here are three reasons that you should be more confident than fearful:

✓ You are educated, trained, and have spent many years associating with hundreds, maybe even thousands of people.

✓ Customers and prospects need products and/or services. They need people like you, or they will fail in their endeavors. So remember they are attending conferences, joining committees, or out socializing for a reason!

✓ Most of us share similar concerns or fears. Take some comfort in knowing that they are people just like us, and they may be hoping you say hello first.

THE REFERRAL: BE "THE CONNECTOR"

Referral

the act of connecting a potential customer who has specific business needs to a sales professional who has a specific solution for those business needs.

By now you have a fairly good idea of how to network and prospect, where to potentially network and prospect, and insight into developing an effective value proposition. This is a terrific start to networking and prospecting, but it doesn't end here. As you network and prospect, you will naturally learn a lot about people and their business. You will also find yourself with the opportunity to refer business to friends you have made in your network. A **referral** is the act of connecting a potential customer who has specific business needs to a sales professional who has a specific solution for those business needs. We all have given a "referral" at one time or another. For example, directing a student to the financial aid office, or recommending your dentist to a friend, or suggesting a landscaper/painter/plumber all constitute a referral. One of the most significant behaviors you can deploy early in your professional selling career is to be a connector in the business community and referral source for your network. You will find that the more you refer business to others, the more they will be inclined to support you as well.

Think of a mortgage loan officer and a realtor. One professional provides home loans, and the other professional sells houses. This is a perfect referral opportunity. Let's assume you were the mortgage loan officer who qualified a young couple to buy a home. Then you refer that same couple to your favorite realtor to find a house to buy. Who do you think the realtor will send his/her customers to when they need financing? You will not only receive referrals from the realtor, but you will have the added leverage to ASK the realtor to please keep your bank in mind for more home loans. On the flipside, imagine cold-calling a random realtor, and asking him/her if they knew anybody looking for a home loan. This method of cold calling is less effective than proactively referring business first. It's not hard to figure out that if you refer business first you will have others in your network sending you referrals as well. This is also a smart concept to discuss in your job interviews! Hiring managers look for these behaviors.

CHAPTER SUMMARY

Networking is like running the 12-minute mile, whereas Prospecting is like running the 6-minute mile. Both will eventually pay off, but knowing the fundamental difference between these two concepts will make you a far more efficient sales representative—or—a far more effective sales manager who can spot the difference and provide coaching. Networking is your ability to meet members of the business community who may provide influence in the industry you work in. As your network grows, a sales professional

©German S/Shutterstock.com

will be more effective in prospecting former or new customers. There are many ways to network with business professionals, and ultimately to locate a potential prospect. One way to network is to identify relevant trade shows and conferences, but only the ones that are being attended by the people you want to do business with. Other ways to network and prospect are to join relevant committees, state local and state functions, volunteer at your local schools and sports programs, or host your own networking event! But remember, getting to these venues is only half the battle. Once you are relevant in these venues, people WILL ask what it is you do, and what it is you will do for them. Therefore, we highly recommend developing an effective, specific value proposition that allows you to sum up what it is you do for a career, and what it is you will do for the customers. It's one of the biggest mistakes college graduates make when a prospective employer asks "Why should I hire you?" A value proposition is something every college graduate entering business should have memorized.

Lastly, a referral is a good way to practice being a connector in the business community. As you are out meeting hundreds and potentially thousands of people in your career you will have many opportunities to connect customers with businesses in your network. This is a behavior we recommend you deploy early in your professional selling career, because it will boomerang back and pay you tenfold!

REFERENCES

Sweeney Group. https://www.coursehero.com/file/p70ibgd/According-to-a-Sweeney-Group-definition-CRM-is-all-the-tools-technologies-and/

Tousley, Scott J. 2017. "107 Mind-Blowing Sales Statistics That Will Help You Sell Smarter." https://blog.hubspot.com/sales/sales-statistics#sm.0001270sszdh0f7nyto1rle8zs4a1

4 HOMEWORK

JT and three of his sales representatives were scheduled to attend the 20th Annual Dental Conference in Dallas. This conference was the biggest of the year for JT and his team, and this would arguably be their best opportunity to network. Upon arriving at the conference, the four of them attended the networking mixer in the corner ballroom. They did not recognize anybody from the conference so they sat at the same table conveniently located in the middle of the ballroom. About thirty minutes later the room became full and the bar area became packed. Again, not recognizing anybody, JT and his team sat idle. Seeing a need to get his team active, JT suggested, "Hey, I'll head to the bar and get us a drink. Anybody want anything?" Two of them asked for a soda, and the other two requested a glass of wine.

While at the bar, one of JT's top five clients recognized JT and said, "JT! What in the world are you doing here? I had no idea you were coming to this conference. Are you here alone?" JT pointed to his team sitting in the middle of the room and said, "No, I am not here alone. I'm with my sales team. How are you, Chuck? I had no idea you were attending this conference either."

Chuck waved to JT's team and said, "Well, I'm going to grab a drink and say hello to a few folks. What are you going to do JT?"

JT shrugged and said, "I am going to grab my team a drink as well, and we are going to hang out for a while and see if we recognize anybody." Chuck put his arm around JT and said, "That's great, JT. Maybe I can buy you a drink later? Great seeing you."

JT smiled and nodded in agreement. After JT ordered his drinks he noticed that Chuck was still standing next to him and apparently having a difficult time ordering from the bartender. "Chuck, do you want me to get the bartender for you?" JT asked. Chuck shook his head signifying "no thanks." JT went back to his table and handed each team member their respective drink.

Approximately forty-five minutes later another one of JT's clients, Tom Moran, approached the table and said, "Hey guys, when did you arrive in town? I didn't know if I would see anybody from your company at this conference." One of JT's sales representatives replied, "Oh we come every year. I'm Tracy, and I report to JT. I cover the California territory for our company. Nice to meet you." Tom walked around the table and shook Tracy's hand and said, "California? I did not know you guys covered California. My company opened three new facilities in San Diego. You have a business card?" Tracy said that he forgot his business cards, but he will get Tom's contact info from JT in the coming weeks and will be in touch. After a few more minutes of pleasantries, Tom parted ways and the networking event was slowly coming to a close.

QUESTION 1: From a Networking and Sales perspective, what areas of concern do you see with JT and his sales team at this conference?

QUESTION 2: What could JT and his sales team have done in advance of the conference to prepare for more effective networking?

CHAPTER 5
Effective Communications

The most valuable of all talents is that of never using two words when one will do.

— *Thomas Jefferson*

©woaiss/Shutterstock.com

CHAPTER OBJECTIVES

- ✓ Discuss common misunderstandings of communications

- ✓ The Art of Communicating UP

- ✓ The Art of Communicating DOWN (great perspective for aspiring sales managers!)

- ✓ Learn effective communication techniques

- ✓ Discuss how Non-Verbal Communication can be a terrific asset in communications, but can also be widely misinterpreted

Baylor Electric and Plumbing was established in 1995 with one location and three employees. By 2017, and after carving out a niche market of mid-size commercial clients, Baylor Electric and Plumbing grew to thirteen offices in ten states, annual revenues of $20 million, and 300 employees.

Brad Swenson, the Chief Operating Officer of Baylor Electric and Plumbing, had an exciting meeting with the company's CFO and CEO. It appears the company's Board of Directors has tasked the CEO with growing revenues by 20 percent in 2018. Furthermore, after consulting with the CEO and CFO, the leaders concluded that in order to achieve 20 percent in new revenues they will need approximately thirty new employees in varying sectors of the company. The leadership team had no doubt that the current employees would welcome the good news. Higher revenues and thirty new hires meant that many employees would have opportunities for promotions, lateral transfers, improved value to the employee ESOP, and so on.

The leadership team decided that one of the ways to set the stage for growth in 2018 was to become more efficient with the company's current resources. For example, the first opportunity they identified was the use of corporate cars in each of its thirteen locations. Corporate cars were used by employees for business meetings and travel within 150 miles of the office. A quick inventory of corporate cars showed that the company had forty corporate-owned cars, with some offices having as many as five in their parking lot. Commercial liability insurance for these cars was costing the company approximately $250,000 a year. This did not include basic maintenance, registration, and other costs associated with owning forty cars. Nonetheless, access to company cars was always considered a "perk" of working at Baylor Electric and Plumbing, and many of the old-timers took the cars home at night.

©Rawpixel.com/Shutterstock.com

Brad decided to send out a memo to the managers in each of the thirteen offices letting them know the company was poised to grow, had the support of the Board and CEO, and new opportunities would flourish in 2018. He also articulated in the memo that in order to grow, the company would need to reallocate resources. Therefore, effective next month, there will be no more company cars. However, if an employee needed a car for business purposes, they may rent a car—pending approval from their supervisor. Two days later Brad sent out another memo to the office managers stating that employees were no longer allowed to book a business trip or conference without using the company's newly installed "trip planning software." The new trip planning software searched for the cheapest flights, most reasonable hotels, as well as alerts for discounts to upcoming conferences. Additionally, since this new software was tied to a successful travel agency, the corporate office would be incented redeemable points and financial incentives on a tier basis. Brad reiterated that this was not only an efficient system for everybody in the company, but employees would no longer unintentionally overpay when booking airline flights or expensive hotels. Accounting estimated that this would save the company an additional $75,000 per year. Without question, these new announcements would save the company a lot of money and allow the leadership team to invest these savings in new people, software, and market share.

Within forty-five days of the announcements six veteran employees resigned or retired prematurely. As they exited the company they began to spread rumors that the company was becoming too corporate, too greedy, too conservative with its resources, and the company culture was clearly shifting in the wrong direction. After all, employees now had to ask permission to rent a car and fill out paperwork explaining why, what for, when, and for how long. "What's next? No more coffee in the offices? That will save them another $100 per month," an office manager was heard complaining.

To make matters worse, several of the employees who resigned started their own companies, and actively recruited several of Baylor Electric and Plumbing's best employees. The news of resignations, company unrest, and rumors disappointed the senior manager team. The leadership team felt they were making excellent choices, avoiding wasteful spending, becoming efficient with resources, and setting the company up for growth and opportunity. The CEO asked Brad what he thought went wrong. Brad's response was, "You would think they would have welcomed the news. Maybe we could have communicated the policy changes differently. Perhaps a memo was perceived as too cold and too corporate. The intention was never to take things away from people, nor was it to cause any disruption in how they conduct their business. Maybe I should have visited with each of the office managers in person, or by phone, and allowed them to ask questions in advance of the announcements. Perhaps this would have helped the managers to better understand the significance of these changes. Perhaps explaining WHY we were making the changes and HOW this would impact the company's ESOP and growth potential would have helped avoid the negativity."

CLASS EXERCISE

Please take 3–5 minutes and discuss what steps Brad Swenson could take in the future to avoid miscommunication. Consider these two questions in your discussion: (1) Were the corporate leaders acting in good faith by making these changes? (2) Can you understand or empathize with WHY the employees heard a different message?

In *How to Win Friends & Influence People,* Dale Carnegie (1998) says that approximately 90 percent of all management problems stem from miscommunication. In the story of Baylor Electric and Plumbing this is an excellent case study of corporate miscommunications. Think about it: employees could still rent cars as needed, and were still allowed to book trips as needed. The fundamentals of using corporate cars and travel were not altered. Nonetheless, the employees heard a different message: corporate was making sweeping changes and the times were changing. What was quickly gained in newly allocated company resources was now lost in

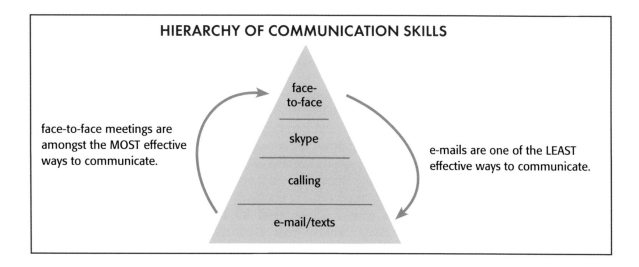

the disappearance of intellectual capital, office disruption, unsubstantiated rumors, and lower employee morale.

Miscommunication happens in business every day, as well as our personal lives. Many times these miscommunications come without a single uttered word, but are heard loud and clear through nonverbal communication. In this chapter we will dive into the root of miscommunications—both verbal and non-verbal. We will work with each of you (those aspiring to go into professional selling, and those who aspire to manage people) to become more aware of what you say, how you say it, and the potential impact that communication can have on your professional selling career.

CLASS EXERCISE

Please take 3–5 minutes and discuss the hierarchy:

1. What advantage does someone making a phone call have over someone sending an e-mail/text in this hierarchy?
2. What advantage does someone using Skype/Zoom have over someone making a phone call in this hierarchy?
3. What advantage does someone have in a face-to-face meeting over someone having a meeting through skype?

Note: please discuss this question as a class: Generally speaking, we seem to all admit it is best to get in front of a client versus sending e-mails. If someone has more advantages as the hierarchy goes UP, then why is it that many of us tend to communicate through e-mails/texts as a society? And for those of you considering sales management someday, do you have any recommendations on training your staff to make them more aware of effective communication methods?

FIVE WAYS TO COMMUNICATE MORE EFFECTIVELY

1. Ask the right questions.

In Chapter 2 we discussed effective listening skills, questioning methods, and introduced the ODRE process (Open questions, Directive questions, Reflective questions, and Earning Commitment). With the ODRE process, you start by asking broad questions in order to understand the big picture, but then you strategically begin to ask more specific and reflective questions to understand the impact to the customer and their business. After you understand the impact to the company and the individuals, you are now positioned to earn a commitment for the next meeting—or potentially closing the deal. Think of your experience with a doctor. They start by asking you a series of questions: "Does it hurt when you do this? Are you exercising on a weekly basis? When you cough, is it productive or dry?" Doctors start out asking broad questions, but eventually make their way directly to the symptoms, and ultimately a solution for your medical condition. A professional sales representative should view themselves in the same light as a doctor: never meet a potential prospect without having an effective questioning process in place.

Dr. Lund was quoted in *Forbes* as saying when someone else communicates with us, the way we interpret their message is based on the following three things (Anderson 2013):

- ✓ 55% is based on their facial expressions and their *body language*.

- ✓ 37% is based on the tone of their voice.

- ✓ 8% is based on the words they say.

---

2. Know the audience.

Lawyers, accountants, human resource professionals, and engineers are very detail-oriented professions. As a result these professionals tend to ask a lot of questions and appreciate as much detail as possible. On the other hand, CEO's, CMO's, Business Development Managers, and many sales professionals tend to be "big picture" people. As a result, they may not want all of the details, nor do they require too much information. A CEO said to me once, "I don't care about all of the data, just show me where the new opportunities are." Myers Briggs and other professional consulting firms specialize in personality testing to decipher the full range of personalities in any given company. Many professional selling positions require personality testing before hiring to ensure the candidate has a penchant for socializing and meeting people. These tests can be a useful tool in hiring the right personalities, but they are also a useful tool in helping a manager engage his/her employees. Just think of a marketing department: one employee in the department is a graphics designer; a detailed-oriented artist who appreciates every color scheme, every corner, and every detail of a marketing brochure. Whereas, another employee—the business development manager—is an outgoing personality who cares much less about the details of a brochure and much more about socializing with people and developing long-term relationships. Each of these personalities may report to one manager, so you can clearly see how miscommunication and misinterpretations can occur. It may be wise for a new college graduate to take one of these professional personality tests. It may be equally as wise for aspiring sales managers to think about different personalities, and how to communicate to a diverse team. Understanding your own personality style may provide a good segue into understanding the many personalities of others.

CLASS EXERCISE

Break up into groups of five. Each group represents a marketing department in a regionally based company. This marketing department is tasked with managing all of the logistics for a pending open house celebration. The open house will be a ribbon-cutting for a new facility opening in Phoenix, Arizona. The company is expecting upward of 250 members of the business community, and this will include several city officials such as the mayor and city council. Later this week, the CFO of the company would like to speak with you regarding an update on the open house. Additionally, the CEO has also requested that you swing by her office and provide a status report as well. Each executive has allotted you approximately ten minutes to give your updates. **Your group is to discuss for five to seven minutes on what your report to the CFO will entail, and what your report to the CEO will entail. Additionally, based on this chapter thus far, are there any effective questions or inquiries that you could ask of the CFO and CEO in advance to help you prepare for the ten-minute briefing?

3. The art of Communicating UP.

One of the main reasons we hear young professionals quit their employers in the first 12 months is due to the growing pressure from their immediate supervisor. As a new graduate and professional early in his/her career it is smart business practice to learn how to communicate "up" to your supervisor—or, perhaps even more importantly—how to communicate interdepartmentally. Upon starting your new career, the authors highly recommend asking your supervisor a very simple question: "How do you like to be communicated with?" For example: do they prefer e-mail, phone call, or face time? How *frequently* do they prefer reports or updates? Every week? Every month? If so, what day? And lastly, when you provide information or a report, how much detail do they want to see? Do they want a brief summary touching on the key points? Or, do they want the who, what, when, why, and how much? By asking these questions upfront you are taking proactive steps to communicate effectively with your supervisor. The authors call this an in-flight correction: when a plane is off just 2 degrees, it is not a big deal for the moment, or for the next 3–5 minutes. However, in about 30 minutes—if uncorrected—the plane is WAY off course, and it becomes a big problem. Try to view engaging your boss as in-flight corrections. If you are slightly off base for a week or two, it's better to have an in-flight correction at THAT time versus a major correction during the 6-month performance review! Just remember one tip: Regardless of how your supervisor prefers to be communicated to, it is still highly recommended to spend some face time with him/her when possible.

FIVE TIPS FOR COMMUNICATING UP:

✓ E-mails and text messages have a high probability of interpretation (or **MIS**interpretation)

✓ If you e-mail or text, proofread to ensure no grammatical errors

✓ Always ask if your superior is comfortable with your update/ report

✓ Face to face is the most recommended form of communicating with your superiors

✓ Avoid lengthy time gaps of communication with your supervisor. When in doubt, a call to "check in" is highly recommended

---

4. The art of Communicating DOWN.

Some of you will graduate and have the good fortune of entering a management training program in which you will find yourselves managing staff early in your career. Some of you may already be managing people right now. And if you are already on the management track, you likely have additional responsibilities communicating with other department heads in your organization, your superiors, and customers. A good discipline to implement when communicating with employees is to listen first, empathize, and then respond accordingly. Let's review each phase:

LISTEN FIRST

Employees are a company's greatest assets. Without good employees it is difficult to run an effective business, especially in professional selling because the employees deal with customers. By listening to your employees you send the message that their point of view is the first order of business. For example, in a weekly sales meeting a good practice is to begin the meeting by allowing the representative to talk about his or her week. A manager may set the boundaries (i.e., "What's working? What's not working? And how can I help?"). However, it is good practice to allow the employee the opportunity to share his/her perspective on the week prior. The employee might have had a poor performance this week, but there may have been reasons outside of their control (such as a top customer moving out of state and closing their account). If the manager begins the meeting with assumptions, such as "Hey Bob, I noticed your numbers dropped this week and you are not yourself lately," an employee may become defensive, angry, embarrassed, or simply surprised you are targeting him/her.

COMMUNICATION

Similar in an employee performance review, a good communication tactic is to start by asking the employee to rate their own performance first. If the manager begins the evaluation by saying, "Bob, your numbers have dropped lately. What's going on?" the employee may feel the manager is out to get them and doesn't understand the big picture. However, if the manager began the meeting with "Bob, how do YOU think you are performing this past quarter?" the manager may hear that it was a slow quarter—but—this past month was his best in five years. The trend is clearly heading in the right direction! By listening to the employee's point of view first it sends the message that the manager is taking the time to understand and not assume.

EMPATHIZE

Emotional Intelligence

the capacity to be aware of, control, and express one's emotions, and to handle interpersonal relationships judiciously and empathetically.

Emotional intelligence is your ability to put yourself in someone else's shoes and empathize with their situation—whether you agree with them or not. There is a story of Abraham Lincoln just after the Civil War. A Confederate soldier came to the White House after the war and asked the President to pardon him. The President empathized with the clearly fatigued soldier, pardoned him, and sent him on his way. Shocked by what they just witnessed, a staff member at the White House said to President Lincoln, "Mr. President, we just spent the last four years of our lives at war against the Confederates. We finally win the war, and now you pardon their soldiers?" To this the President responded, "If I was born in the South I would have probably been fighting alongside of them. He has asked for forgiveness, so I pardoned him. It is time to heal as a country and move forward."

After listening to your employees, an effective communication tactic is to show empathy for what you just heard. For example, perhaps an employee reports that her numbers are down, but she has a reasonable explanation: two of her top clients have moved out of state and closed their accounts. By listening first, and THEN empathizing that these circumstances were clearly out of her control, the manager can then respond with advice on how to move forward. The truth is, despite this situation being out of her control, her numbers are down and they cannot stay down forever (or much longer). However, how you communicate this message could be the difference in a resentful employee—or—an employee who feels that she has the understanding and support of her manager.

RESPOND

It's one thing for an employee to have the understanding and support of his/her manager, but at the end of the day a manager has a fiduciary duty to drive high performance, results, and ultimately shareholder value. Let's assume you mastered the first two steps in communicating effectively: you listened, and you empathized. You will now be in an excellent position to communicate with employees what steps he/she must *now* take to improve the current situation. One method to respond and communicate is the use of a Performance Improvement Plan (PIP). A PIP is a document that allows the manager and the employee to clearly state the situation and what steps will be taken to *improve* the situation. An effective PIP will have goals, strategies to meet those goals, and firm dates to manage the progress. Without listening and empathizing, a PIP can be perceived by the employee as being in hot water with the boss.

Let's take the example in the above section in which the employee lost two of her top clients. High performing sales professionals desire to win and grow their business. Chances are that this sales representative is already in poor spirits as a result of her clients closing their accounts. In sales, there is very little time to fret or worry about a lost client or declining revenues. Time is of the essence, and this employee may **need** a manager to jump in and help figure out a path forward. If the manager does not have clear methods of communicating DOWN to his or her employees, it can become a very difficult situation for the manager to help, and the lack of effective communication techniques can result in this employee failing to overcome the current situation.

DID YOU KNOW

✓ "People with average IQs outperform those with the highest IQs 70% of the time." (Bradberry, Greaves, and Lencioni)

---

5. *The art of closing the loop with your clients.*

A professional sales representative will likely have many clients and prospects. These clients and prospects will have many questions as a result of

New-Task Buying Situation

when decision-makers perceive the problem or need as totally different from previous experiences; therefore, they need a significant amount of information to explore alternative ways of solving the problem and searching for alternative suppliers.

Influentials

any person(s) who have direct impact on the chief decision-maker and his/her ability to finalize a decision.

a **new-task buying situation** in which they may need a significant amount of information before deciding to purchase. Or the clients and prospects may have an *expectation* that you will communicate in a manner that will help alleviate some of their anxiety resulting from the pending purchase.

There are a couple ways to address "closing the loop" with a buyer. **First**, it is recommended to simply ask the buyer or prospect what concerns they have—even if they have not previously shared any concerns with you. By asking what concerns they may have you are: (1) building trust by asking thoughtful questions, and (2) proactively uncovering potential objections that may be lingering just below the surface. **Second**, once they communicate what concerns they have, it is highly recommended you write them down in your notepad, and then repeat back what you heard them say. For example, "So if I am hearing you correctly, you have two concerns: (1) justifying this purchase to your senior management team, and (2) how this payroll software will be implemented in the middle of a busy week. Am I hearing you correctly? And is there anything else I may be missing?"

By closing the loop you have now positioned yourself to either address these concerns on the spot—or—find out what it *will* take to help the buyer overcome his/her concerns. For example, perhaps a follow-up meeting that includes **influentials** in the buying process—such as the buyer's boss, or CFO, or leadership team may set the stage for company "buy in." In fact, if this purchase is NEW to the client/company you should expect many other influentials to weigh in and ask questions—so be prepared on all fronts! The art of closing the loop can be best simplified by your ability to ask the right questions, answer the questions, and then confirm that these concerns are no longer an issue in the decision-making process. If the buyer says that he/she is still not comfortable, it very likely means you have not adequately uncovered their concerns. In these cases, it may be wise to strategize with your manager to figure out next "best" steps.

Closing the loop can be an excellent behavior that you talk about in a job interview—or—a behavior you deploy in your professional selling career.

ETHICAL

Jacquie is a sales professional of high-end data and software solutions for enterprise business. This role entails supporting her B2B clients from the desktop all the way to the data center. One of Jacquie's major accounts, MX-Gen, has been working on roadmap transition for the past year which entails a five-year strategy to upgrade its network into a cutting-edge communication platform. This state-of-the-art "designed and sold" solution by Jacquie's team will bring the customer experience to one unified platform across all of its communication channels. For example, web chat, contact center agent calling, e-mailing, and texting, will be a single omnichannel relationship that will afford their employees the same user experience from any digital device, IOS, or any technology-based communication tools that the customer prefers to work from.

This solution has an expected budget of $65m+ over the term. At this point the project is 30 percent complete. If this roadmap is successful their

©antoniodiaz/Shutterstock.com

company could potentially be branded as "THE JD Power" award winner for Customer Service—a truly remarkable honor.

Jacquie's regional VP Manager, Cecilia, was set to attend the company's upcoming sales conference, and therefore took the initiative to schedule some face time with a few members of Jacquie's sales team. At the coffee shop in the hotel lobby Cecilia opened the conversation with a question regarding the MX-Gen account project. She was particularly interested in the project forecasting, expected next order, and professional services billing. After a brief summary by Jacquie's team, Cecilia realizes that the core hardware manufacturer for the MX-Gen project is a current business partner who is going through a major reorganization of their company, and possibly a Chapter 11 bankruptcy. In other words, a significant piece of the project that they have been pitching to the client may now be in jeopardy. Cecilia gathers her thoughts and decides that her sales team needs to have a quick and decisive strategy on what should be communicated and how much of this emerging information needs to be shared with MX-Gen . . . the impacts around pending orders, in-process design service and support issues, as well as the contractual impacts to all parties, manufacturer to MX-Gen.

- ✓ Should we communicate this with the customer?

- ✓ When and what should we communicate to the customer?

- ✓ Do we have a duty to speak to the manufacturer first?

- ✓ What are the options? Do we, and should we, communicate that?

©Aila Images/Shutterstock.com

Please discuss three different ways this non verbal signal "can" be interpreted.

NON-VERBAL COMMUNICATION

Non-verbal communication is one of the most risky forms of communication and almost entirely up to interpretation by others. UCLA's Professor Emeritus of Psychology, Dr. Mehrabian, coined the 8%–37%–55% rule: words account for 8%, tone of voice accounts for 37%, and body language accounts for 55% (Mehrabian 1971). So that means that 92 percent of communication is nonverbal. Please draw your attention to the picture to the right. There are several ways this non-verbal gesture could be interpreted or (misinterpreted) by the receiving party.

Most of us are not aware of our non-verbal behaviors. For example, some people smile and giggle when they are nervous. Others may stare at the ground when they are processing serious information. The secret to non-verbal communication is that your body language should be aligned with your words. If the two are misaligned, the gap for misinterpretation widens! If you have a tendency to mock others, roll your eyes, and use body language to complement your verbal messages, it may be wise to distance yourself from these non-verbal behaviors early on in your career.

According to Northeastern University Professor, Dr. Edward G. Wertheim, non-verbal communication can play any one of five roles in your daily business:

- ✓ **Repetition:** body gestures can reflect or repeat what the other person is attempting to communicate.

- ✓ **Contradiction:** gestures can be contradictory to what the other person is saying or communicating.

- ✓ **Substitution:** a gesture can substitute for a verbal message. For example, a person's wide eyes can signify the seriousness of a conversation.

- ✓ **Complementing:** non-verbal messages may complement a verbal message. For example, a boss who fist-bumps an employee in addition to giving praise can add to the verbal impact of the message.

- ✓ **Accenting:** they may accent or compliment a verbal message. For example, hitting the table with your fist can underscore that you are not only serious, but angry as well. (Wertheim n.d.)

CHAPTER SUMMARY

Some research indicates that 90 percent of all management problems stem from poor communication. Getting in the room with a client will dramatically improve your chances of success. The same holds true with interviewing for a job: don't just e-mail your resume and cross your fingers; rather, call the company and see if you can arrange a meeting with the hiring manager(s). We offer you five ways to approach improving your communication right now: (1) true professionals know how to prepare questions, and the most successful sales professionals never go into a business meeting without knowing what questions to ask. (2) Know your audience. Sounds obvious, but we sometimes communicate to a CFO the same way as we talk to our business development manager. Lawyers, accountants, doctors, and engineers tend to want/need *more* information with a *lot* of detail. CEO's, business development managers, and sales professionals tend to appreciate "the big picture" with *less* emphasis on the details. By knowing your audience (and appreciating their preferred method of communication) you will have a greater success communicating, especially in those early years in your career. (3) Communicating UP is an art, not a science. The authors highly recommend that you ask your superiors *how* they like communication to flow. Do they prefer a once a week face-to-face meeting? Do they like daily updates by e-mail? By understanding how your superiors appreciate information to flow you will greatly minimize miscommunication, and you will likely increase the level of trust in the relationship. There are personality tests that are good tools to further understand your personality and communication strengths/weakness. (4) Some of you will enter management training programs, or inherit a sales team early on in your career. The authors recommend you deploy the three steps of communicating DOWN: always listen first, show empathy, and respond accordingly. Many times responding means jumping in to help your sales representative. One way we suggested to "jump in and help" is to use a Performance Improvement Plan (PIP) that is designed to address the challenge(s), and define a road map of action items to help the sales representative get back on the right track. But be careful, this third step can be a difficult and onerous process if you did not implement the first two steps: listening and empathizing. (5) Always close the loop with your customers. Too often we are busy selling and not paying attention to their concerns. A simple call to your customer saying, "I took care of that order for you, and it will be there in 5 days," is one way to let the buyer know the loop has been closed.

In this chapter we lay out a two-step technique of closing the loop: (1) Ask if there are any concerns, and (2) Repeat back what you heard so that the buyer gets a clear picture that you heard them and that you do understand the issues. If you execute these first two steps correctly, you will find that you are not only positioned to address concerns, but that subtle objections (such as buy-in from influentials) can be addressed as well. As a sales professional, you will now be positioned to not only close the loop with a client, but close the deal as well!

Lastly, research shows that non-verbal communication (body language and the tone of your voice) can account for upward of 92 percent of your communication with others. A simple awareness of your own non-verbal behaviors is a great start, but the key is to have non-verbal language that *aligns* with the meaning of your spoken words. Otherwise, you may be disproportionally misunderstood. Working on these behaviors will give you a competitive advantage in your career.

REFERENCES

Anderson, Amy R. 2013. "Successful Business Communication: It Starts At The Beginning." *Forbes* (May 28). https://www.forbes.com/sites/amyanderson/2013/05/28/successful-business-communication-it-starts-at-the-beginning/#4f5d7cf61db5

Bradberry, Travis, Greaves, Jean, and Lencioni, P. M. 2009. *Emotional Intelligence 2.0.* San Diego: TalentSmart.

Carnegie, Dale. 1998. *How to Win Friends & Influence People.* New York: Pocket Books.

Lohrey, Jackie. n.d. "How Communication Affects Productivity Statistics." AZ Central.

Mehrabian, Albert. 1971. *Silent Messages.* Belmont, CA: Wadsworth.

Paton, Cassie. 2015. "7 Surprising Stats That Show the Importance of Internal Communications." Enplug Blog. https://blog.enplug.com/7-surprising-internal-communications-stats

Wertheim, Edward G. n.d. "The Importance of Effective Communication" (PDF). https://www.scribd.com/document/69092770/Effective-Communication

5 HOMEWORK

As the regional sales manager of Matrix Pharmaceutical Supplies, Maxwell Smith oversaw twelve sales representatives who covered a fifteen-state region. Maxwell's division president, Colby Woods, was tasked with communicating with his regional managers in regard to an upcoming national sales meeting. On Monday morning Maxwell received this e-mail memo from his boss, Colby:

> "Good morning Maxwell. As you know Matrix Pharmaceutical Supplies is hosting our 25th Annual Sales Conference in Chicago. Our CEO will be in attendance, and she is looking forward to meeting each member of your sales team. Five members of your team are continuously in her President's Top 10, so this will be a great opportunity for the senior management team to recognize the excellent work you and your terrific sales team have done in recent months. Please RSVP by close of business Friday so we can get the event coordinated and logistics taken care of. My best, Colby Woods."

Maxwell read the e-mail and simply forwarded the memo on to his sales team. His message to the team was: "See below. Let me know if you have questions. Thanks. MS"

Thursday afternoon rolled around and Maxwell received another e-mail from his boss, Colby. This time it read:

> "Maxwell, I realize you and the team are out working and making a huge difference for Matrix Pharmaceutical Supplies. But as of Thursday, 2:00 p.m. Central time, only three members of your entire region have RSVP'd for our 25th Annual Sales Conference. Did you receive my memo on Monday? As you could imagine, I am highly disappointed at the lack of your team's enthusiasm and response, and I would hope that you and the team will revisit my original e-mail (see below e-mail) and reconsider this wonderful opportunity to celebrate our recent success and engage with our CEO. Sincerely, Colby Woods."

Perplexed, and quite frankly caught off guard, Maxwell fired off an e-mail to his team:

> "Team! I just received a memo from our divisional president that *only three employees* from our team have RSVP'd for the annual conference. This is unacceptable, and quite frankly I am embarrassed!!! I need RSVP's from ALL of you by close-of-business tomorrow or I will be withholding quarterly bonuses for a month. I realize you are all busy, but perhaps this e-mail will serve to remind you of the importance of this annual event in Chicago. MS"

QUESTION 1: Who is the MOST responsible for the communication breakdown?

A. The members of the regional sales team. If your boss, and boss's boss e-mail you, the responsibility to respond is yours!

B. Maxwell. He is where the breakdown occurs. Neither his boss or team seem to be happy about the flow of information.

C. Colby. He told everybody to RSVP by close of business Friday. Yet he was complaining before the Friday deadline, and that is not fair to everyone in the e-mail chain.

QUESTION 2: What advice do you have for Maxwell and Colby to communicate more effectively?

CHAPTER 6
Knowing Your Customers

You can have everything in life you want, if you will just help other people get what they want.

— *Zig Ziglar*

©Billion Photos/Shutterstock.com

CHAPTER OBJECTIVES

✓ Discuss the concept that customers do not share the same enthusiasm of a company (or a professional sales representative representing the company)

✓ Understand the importance of researching a business and its industry before meeting with clients

✓ Develop tangible and practical methods for researching industries, companies, and decision-makers prior to a sales meeting

✓ Discuss the various tools that allow a professional sales representative to continuously learn about his/her customers

✓ Review well-researched insights for choosing optimal times to communicate with a client

In 2012, Lou D'Amico had decided to open his own business as a marketing and communications consultant. And for good reason! Lou had just spent the previous five years as the chief marketing officer for one of the largest, most diversified engineering companies in the United States. In that capacity he oversaw the company's internal and external marketing, sales initiatives, public relations, and communications. He was also the chief community liaison tasked with market penetration and business development efforts. In a nutshell, Lou was responsible for telling the company's story and creating an awareness and demand that would ultimately help drive new revenues.

Upon launching his consulting business, Lou decided to call on a local, regionally-based hospital that was seemingly losing the public relations fight against a much larger national hospital that recently moved into the community. In an effort to gain immediate market share, this national hospital was spending a fortune on marketing efforts and community relations. With some quick research into the smaller, locally-based hospital, Lou was able to decipher that they did have a marketing director who oversaw the local marketing efforts, but they lacked the staff and resources to compete against the newly arrived national giant. Lou felt that a consultant with local, regional, and national marketing and communications expertise might be a service that the local hospital was willing to consider on a short-term, contract basis.

©wavebreakmedia/Shutterstock.com

Lou decided to call the president of the local hospital and see if a meeting could be set to discuss this potential consulting partnership. After two short voicemails explaining who he was and an overview of his experience Lou did not receive a call back from the local hospital. He decided that perhaps an e-mail to the president may prove more effective. In the e-mail, Lou once again introduced himself as a marketing and communications professional who provided expert consulting services on a contract basis. He laid out the highlights of his past experience assisting corporations, particularly with respect to competing for market share. Lou pointed out that the new hospital was indeed making a big splash in the community and that perhaps he could assist the local hospital in protecting their market share.

He was right, within a few short days the president of the hospital wrote an e-mail back: "Dear Mr. D'Amico, thank you for the e-mail. Although you have articulated very well what it is you do, it is clear to me that you have not taken the time to understand what it is we do, or what our short- and long-term objectives are with respect to the new national hospital that has recently come to town. We are a smaller hospital and have historically experienced a 90 percent patient retention rate. Since the new national hospital arrived last year that number has actually improved to 92 percent. It has become evident that our patients prefer our local presence and personal attention from our staff (who do a terrific job, as you can see from the retention rates). The community seems unmoved by the new competitor's marketing blitz, press releases, and many other community tactics that you have highlighted in your e-mail. Therefore, as an administration we do not see a business need to add new marketing staff or consultants at this time. While I appreciate you reaching out, in the future I would suggest discovering what your potential clients need first before selling what it is you have to offer. I am sorry, but at this time we are headed in a completely different direction with our marketing efforts. Again, thank you for reaching out."

KNOWING YOUR CUSTOMERS

As professional salespeople, we tend to be confident, outgoing, and passionate about our products or services. It is natural for professional salespeople to believe that their customers share that same enthusiasm when purchasing our products or services. However, recent research by Bain & Company demonstrates a startling and sober reality: out of more than 360 firms surveyed, 80 percent believed that their customers were receiving a "superior" experience; yet only 8 percent of the customers surveyed said that their experience was "superior" (Allen, Reichheld, and Hamilton 2005). This research indicates that there can be a massive disconnect between what a company believes is a superior experience versus what the customer believes is superior experience. The customer experience can be impacted any time between when you first meet them, to the sale of the product or service, to long after the sale is closed. So let's look at various ways to get to know your customers and improve your relationship with them.

FIVE WAYS TO GET TO *KNOW YOUR CUSTOMERS*

1. *Know the industry that your customer operates in.*

As you can see from the chapter's opening story, Lou D'Amico did not do proper research or due diligence with regard to the health care industry. In fact, he assumed that one hospital's marketing efforts was more effective than the local, smaller hospital's marketing efforts. Little did he know that the smaller hospital was already closely monitoring their patients and how each patient was responding to the newly arrived competition. A quick review of the health care industry and its trends would have shown Mr. D'Amico that the "patient experience" is where hospitals place a great deal of administrative and marketing resources (not extra billboards, magazine ads, and press releases). The patient experience may include everything from how the patient walks into the main entry of a hospital, to the experience in the waiting area and checking in for appointments, to how the staff treats the patient, to billing the patient long after they have left the hospital (among many other patient experiences). These are all very important administrative and marketing goals for competitive hospitals. For example, some hospitals invest in their websites and communication tools to alert a patient in advance if the doctor or staff is running more than thirty to forty-five minutes behind schedule. Many patients appreciate this advanced notice/information because they can either reschedule the appointment or work the delay into their personal schedule. By researching an industry, the trends impacting the industry, and where the industry is placing its focus may provide tremendous value to a professional sales representative who is trying to make that first sales call.

FIVE WAYS YOU CAN RESEARCH THE INDUSTRY

1. By Location: American Fact Finder

   a. Website: https://factfinder.census.gov

   b. Allows you to search US census data by location, age, income, race, and so forth (Cost: Free)

2. By Segment: Nielsen's MyBestSegments

   a. Website: https://segmentationsolutions.nielsen.com/mybestsegments/

   b. Allows you to research by segment (Cost: Free)

3. General: Google's Marketer's Almanac

   a. Website: https://www.thinkwithgoogle.com/

   b. Allows you to research consumer behavior, and how the behaviors change by the season (Cost: Free)

4. Economic Data: Business Dynamic Statistics

   a. Website: https://www.census.gov/ces/dataproducts/bds/

   b. Allows you to leverage economic data to research new businesses, businesses who shut down, business expansions, and so forth (Cost: Free)

5. By Industry: First Research

   a. Website: www.firstresearch.com

   b. Allows for excellent preparation for sales calls and business planning (Cost: $2,175)

---

2. _Know the company_ or business that you are targeting.

As a rule of thumb, it is smart business to keep abreast of your customers' relevant industries and the trends that impact their behavior. But once that process has been adequately completed, the time has come to spend some time researching the specific company you are targeting. Many times a simple review of a website will reveal which services the company offers, who are the key leaders in the organization, facility locations, and more. Depending on the level of financial or human resources a company places into their public website there are occasions in which locating pertinent information is not easy to find. In those circumstances one recommendation is to try the "contact us" link on the website. Occasionally companies will put the names and contact information of their business development managers or marketing team representatives. These gatekeepers are usually happy to take a phone call or receive an e-mail, and they may point you in the right direction and provide key contact information for the company's decision-makers.

Another method for learning more about a company is through their social media sites (if applicable). For example, Mayo Clinic is one of the world's most renowned and prestigious hospitals. Their Facebook page has an editorial calendar that is well thought out in advance, professionally managed and executed, and provides valuable insight into what is happening at the Mayo Clinic on a weekly and monthly basis (i.e., Nurses Week, Cancer Awareness Month, Job Openings, moving stories about the patient experience, and much more).

Level-Setting

Level-Setting: using intelligence from industry and company research to ask the client quality questions that are designed to position the sales representative as an equal in the business discussion, particularly with C-Level executives.

Lastly, many of the same tools for researching the industry are available to research a specific company as well. For example, First Research (firstresearch.com) is an excellent online research tool that helps many sales professionals understand not only what is happening in the industry, but also some valuable intelligence about their clients, their competition, and potential challenges that their customers may face. Companies such as Paycom—a nationally respected payroll and HR technology organization based out of Oklahoma—use First Research as an intelligence-gathering tool to prepare their sales force for sales presentations/meetings and business planning. The data provided in First Research allows sales professionals at Paycom to "level-set" with C-Level decision-makers. **Level-setting** is when a professional sales representative uses intelligence from industry and company research tools to ask the client quality questions that are designed to _position the sales representative as an equal in the business discussion_, particularly when dealing with C-Level executives. For example, when you ask a client, "Do you have any plans this weekend?" you run the risk of the client perceiving you as wasting his/her time. Many decision-makers, especially C-Level executives such as the Chief Financial Officer are extremely busy professionals. However, by asking deeper, broader questions such as "With the complexity of corporate accounting and HR practices changing on a daily basis, are you finding the need for more personalized service along with the payroll and HR software?" Regardless of how young or inexperienced a professional sales representative may be, when he/she asks level-setting questions the client will immediately shift his/her attention to discussing the business, the industry, and answers to your quality questions (and not get bored with talking about his/her plans for the coming weekend).

CLASS EXERCISE

Go to FirstResearch.com and type in "HDR Engineering" (or another business that the professor suggests). What can you tell the class about HDR Engineering? Are they a major or minor player in professional engineering? Who are their major competitors? Is there any intelligence or research offered about the industry with respect to the next one, five, ten years? If you were interviewing for a job with HDR, is there any information provided here that may be of value in your job interview? Discuss as a class.

©Billion Photos/Shutterstock.com

3. *Know the decision-maker and their key influencers.*

A true sales professional never arrives at a sales meeting without having done some research into the decision-maker. If the customer is a new prospect and there is a minimal history between you (the sales professional) and the customer, then a good place to start is LinkedIn. In fact, according to Sales Strategist, Jill Konrath, top sellers use LinkedIn six or more hours per week. LinkedIn is a free online social media site that connects millions of business professionals. One of the first things to do before meeting a new client is to see if any of YOUR LinkedIn network happens to be a connection with the potential client. If so, you just went from a cold lead to a potentially warm lead because you would now have the ability to contact your LinkedIn connection and find out what he or she knows about the mutual connection or client. If one of your connections in LinkedIn actually works at the same company as your client (or one of the decision-maker's previous companies) you may have just gone from a cold/warm lead to a hot lead. Research shows that 84 percent of prospects usually respond to a sales rep when recommended from someone inside the company (Leung 2014). Think about this tactic not only when you enter professional selling as a career, but when you interview for a job as well. Your odds of getting hired for a job dramatically rise if you are recommended from someone inside the organization. LinkedIn is an easy discipline to deploy before any meeting.

Another method for getting to know your customer is to do a quick Google search to see what stories or facts show up in the search. Sometimes you can learn what community service committee, or charity board, or fundraiser that your client is associated with. Many successful business professionals are involved in the community in some way, shape, or form. Finding out their associations is only going to help your first few meetings with the client (it certainly can't hurt knowing who they associate with, and where).

4. *Knowing your customers is a continuous and life-long effort.*

Sometimes the most abused customers are the customers who already bought a product or service from you. Many times professional sales representatives do a wonderful job marketing to a client, selling the product or service, and ultimately closing the deal. But once they become our customers we can sometimes forget to keep in touch with them and earn their business . . . for life! That is, we work so hard to get them in the door (close the deal), but so little at keeping them in the door (for life). One way to *continuously* know your customers and earn their business for life is to simply ask them about their previous experience purchasing from you and your company. Many companies send out surveys to customers (post-purchase process) asking about their experience in the sales cycle/process. But you as a professional sales representative should always want to know how your customers are doing and their experience in purchasing from you. For example, perhaps you (as the professional sales representative) thought the process was smooth and seamless—and that the customer was happy. However, when you ASK the customer in a survey what their experience/perspective was you are surprised to learn that they were nervous, felt uninformed, the machine arrived late, frustrated with the billing, and so forth.

There are many free and accessible online tools such as Survey Monkey (www.surveymonkey.com) and Qualtrics (www.qualtrics.com) that allow a professional sales representative opportunities to monitor the clients experiences, respond quickly, and improve the situation by deploying basic methods such as surveys. Knowing your customers does not stop at the sale. They, too, are influenced by peer pressure, industry trends, and business needs. Make it your discipline to check in at least once every six to eight weeks to ask how the client is doing (this can be a survey one time, a phone call the next). Research indicates that you should check in with a client at least five to eight times per year. And by checking in, you are continuously getting to know your clients and what changes have occurred in their personal and professional lives. Additionally, by continuously getting to know your clients, professional sales representatives have the opportunity to ask for referrals (after all, if the client continues to reaffirm that they are happy

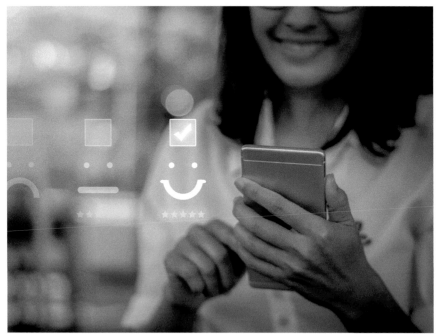

©13_Phunkod/Shutterstock.com

with your service and that things are great, it is reasonable to assume you can ask for referrals from the client). According to the Journal of Marketing, referred customers have a 16 percent higher lifetime value (TeamWave 2016).

5. *Know when is the best TIME—or right time—to call on your customers.*

Communication and connecting with your customers is a critical component of professional selling, especially earlier in the process when the relationship is not strong. Thus far, the textbook discusses methods for HOW to communicate with your customers, but we will now pivot to the concept of WHEN is the optimal time to talk to your customers. For example, if your client is a medical doctor, the best time to call is probably early in the morning before the patients begin to fill the office and occupy the doctor's schedule. There is also significant research that supports not only what TIME of day to call your customers, but what DAY(s) of the week are more effective when contacting your customers. For example, according to the lead response management study, Thursday is a 49.7 percent better day than Tuesday to make contact with a lead over the phone (The Lead Response Management Study, n.d.). Friday is a good day to talk to a customer, but according to the study it is not the highest probability day to obtain a signature or close the deal since many are ready to check out and enjoy the weekend. Having a good sense of who your customers are, what industry they work in, and how their day is impacted, could position you to be more effective in communicating and building relations with your customers.

DID YOU KNOW

✓ The best days for both calling to make contact and calling to qualify are Wednesdays and Thursdays.

✓ The worst day for calling to make contact is Tuesday.

✓ The worst day for calling to qualify a lead is Friday.

Source: The Lead Response Management Study, n.d.

CLASS EXERCISE

PART 1

Choose two students to volunteer. Have one of the students go to the official website of Allegiant Airlines (www.allegiantair.com), and the other student go to the official website of Southwest Airlines (Southwest.com). Once the students arrive on the official landing page, the professor (or other students in the classroom) will time how long it takes each student to find the airline's phone number for making a flight reservation. The two students **are not allowed** to leave the website to find the phone numbers—and—the other students in the classroom are not allowed to assist in this research process. After each student has located the phone number on their respective sites, have the two students explain their experience in searching for each phone number (if the classroom has a projector, perhaps have the student show the class the steps he/she took to locate the phone number). Was it an easy experience? Did one student take much longer than the other student to find the phone number? In your opinion as a potential airline customer, were the websites user-friendly and easy for potential customers to navigate? Discuss as a class.

PART 2

Once Part 1 is complete, using a speaker phone (or any phone/cell phone with a loudspeaker option), have the professor actually call the number you found on the Allegiant Airlines website. The goal is for the professor to actually speak to a live customer service representative to inquire about a round-trip ticket for a trip anywhere within the United States. (Once a live airline customer service representative picks up, you may immediately end the phone call. We are only monitoring how long it takes to get a customer service representative on the phone.) How long did it take to get a live customer service representative on the phone?

Next, repeat the process by calling the phone number you found on the website for Southwest Airlines. Were there differences in the customer experience? Comparing these airlines side by side, do you have any advice for these companies to improve the customer experience? Discuss as a class.

ETHICAL DILEMMA

Dr. Richard Marchese was excited. He just purchased a 2017 Buick Enclave, and it was the first time in ten years that he was able to purchase a "new" car. As he signed the paperwork he could not help but recognize that the process was fairly smooth, the price was reasonable, and the four-year bumper-to-bumper warranty made him feel that this was a good deal. The only thing that bothered Dr. Marchese was that he heard from a friend in his local neighborhood that the same dealership threw in a free auto start device for their 2017 Buick Enclave purchase. But now the dealership would not give the same perk to Dr. Marchese. When Dr. Marchese pressed the sales representative on how come his neighbor received the perk—but not him—the sales representative simply shrugged it off and said they were eager to reach their goal last week, but that deal doesn't apply to everyone all of the time. Dr. Marchese was a little frustrated by this response, but accepted the explanation and decided to buy the car anyway.

Upon walking out of the dealership to his new car, the sales representative said, "I have a coupon for you. It's two free oil changes, but I cannot find it right now. I will call you tomorrow when I find it, and we will get it to you. Thank you, Dr. Marchese, for the business." About a week later Dr. Marchese got a phone call from the sales representative, but to his surprise it was not regarding the coupon for two free oil changes. Instead, the sales representative said, "Hi Dr. Marchese, I hope you have enjoyed the car this past week. I just wanted to let you know that we mailed you out a survey because corporate likes to monitor the experience that all of our customers have when they purchase a new car. If you check 'great experience' in ALL of the boxes on the survey, and you drop it off here at the dealership, I will throw in a free tank of gas for you." This troubled Dr. Marchese, so he asked, "Hey, whatever happened to my coupon for two free oil changes? You said you were going to call me last week, but I never heard from you." The sales representative seemed puzzled and said, "Ya, I'm sorry about that. I thought I could find the coupons but I must have lost them. If they turn up, or I get more coupons from corporate, I will call you." Frustrated, Dr. Marchese hung up the phone. On one hand he wanted to write in the customer survey that he enjoyed the car but did not appreciate the sales professional's inconsistencies. Checking every box with "great

©Rawpixel/Shutterstock.com

experience" did not quite sit right with him. But on the other hand he had to check "great experience" in every box to get a free tank of gas. What should Dr. Marchese do?

A. Fill out the survey, tell corporate everything was great, and take the free gas.

B. Fill out the survey, but be honest with their corporate management team and point out the inconsistencies (after all, the owners have a right to know what REALLY goes on. Free gas is not only costing the owners more money, but it is disingenuous on both the sales professional and Dr. Marchese's part, including Dr. Marchese).

C. Give it a few more days and see if the sales professional locates the coupons for two free oil changes. Perhaps that would ease his frustrations.

D. None of the above. His neighbor got a better deal, and the sales representative never called that next day as promised. What would YOU do?

CHAPTER SUMMARY

The chapter starts off with a situation (based off a true story) about a marketing consultant who failed to convince a local hospital that his expertise could be of value in competing against a larger, national hospital that was new to the area. Put simply, Mr. D'Amico completely misread the landscape, was uninformed of the trends impacting the health care industry, and did not have a thorough understanding of what his client needed. Professional sales consultants will take the time to do their due diligence, research the industry, and know their clients.

There are five recommended ways to improve your ability to know your customers: Know the industry, know the company, know the decision-maker and his/her influence, know how to continuously learn about (and from) your customers, and know the optimal times to connect with your clients. While there are many ways to "know your customers" these five concepts could help launch your career in sales and greatly improve your ramp-up time to success. Just imagine if you interviewed for a medical sales job with a company like GE, and in the interview you walked the hiring manager through these five steps of getting to know your customers. At a minimum, it sets you apart from the other candidates who are also interviewing.

REFERENCES

Allen, James, Reichheld, Frederick, and Hamilton, Barney. 2005. "Tuning into the voice of your customer." Harvard Management Update, October 1. Bain & Company. http://www.bain.com/publications/articles/tuning-into-voice-of-customer.aspx

Kinwith, Jill. https://www.customshow.com/sales-statistics-presentation-data-youll-be-amazed-by/

Leung, Stuart. February 4, 2014. "How to Make a Good Sales Pitch in 7 Steps." Salesforce Blog. https://www.salesforce.com/blog/2014/02/how-to-make-good-sales-pitch.html

TeamWave CRM. April 8, 2016. 50 Amazing Sales Prospecting Stats That Will Improve The Way You Sale. https://blog.teamwave.com/2016/04/08/50-amazing-sales-prospecting-stats-that-will-make-you-a-sales-rock-star/

The Lead Response Management Study. n.d. "The Lead Response Management Study Overview." http://www.leadresponsemanagement.org/lrm_study

6 HOMEWORK

Jimmy Lavin just received a promotion at Rob's Roofing from customer support to lead sales associate. With eight offices in New York City and a name brand that has been around the five boroughs for forty years, Jimmy's earning potential has just sky-rocketed. The promotion came with two weeks of product training and two weeks of sales training. There was a lot to absorb in these four weeks, but in the end Jimmy was ready to get out of the office and find new commercial/residential clients for Rob's Roofing.

Jimmy found the first two months of selling roofing services to be highly discouraging. For starters, he had a difficult time prospecting construction companies. He learned quickly that "construction" meant a lot of things. Some construction companies provided carpentry-only services, while others provided heavy highway construction. He spent several hours each day trying to locate commercial and residential construction companies that needed "roofing" as a contracted service. Another challenge Jimmy faced was understanding the business model of his targeted list. For example, Cheritage Builders is a residential home builder who prided itself on being one of the city's few women-centric custom home builders. With an appeal directly to the female audience, many of the contractors Cheritage partnered with were women-owned. But how was Jimmy supposed to know this before calling on Cheritage? Where would he have learned this fact about the customer and how they operate?

Lastly, even when Jimmy called on his company's list of former clients he was surprised to learn that some of the previous clients had a poor experience with Rob's Roofing. Therefore, the calls were sometimes awkward and caught him off guard.

Jimmy was beginning to feel that he was wasting a lot of time each day, and that maybe sales was not a good fit for him.

QUESTION 1: Can you recommend three ways that Jimmy can become more effective at profiling potential customers? Please explain your reasoning for each answer.

QUESTION 2: What would you recommend Jimmy do before calling on the company's list of "former" clients?

Part Three

Closing the Deal

CHAPTER 7
Overcoming Objection

People don't want to buy a quarter-inch drill. They want a quarter-inch hole.

— *Theodore Levitt,*
Harvard Business School

©iQoncept/Shutterstock.com

CHAPTER OBJECTIVES

✓ A deeper understanding for the reasons why prospects and customers object

✓ Discuss the most common objections that many sales professionals experience daily

✓ Develop a sales discipline that expects and anticipates common objections

✓ Methods for uncovering and overcoming sales objections

It was April in Phoenix, Arizona, and Dain Thomsen decided it was time to get his air conditioners serviced, as he did every April, in anticipation of the summer heat that would inevitably come. Air conditioner serviceman, Jimmy Hall, inspected both of Dain's air conditioner units, and while Mr. Hall said the units were functioning adequately for the time being, they were already fifteen years old and would likely not make it through the summer. In other words, Dain can reasonably expect his air conditioners to break down at any time. This was not a complete surprise to Dain. His air conditioners had already been repaired twice in the past twelve months, and both times the servicemen informed Dain that these air conditioners would not last more than a couple more months. With a wife, three young children, and two dogs at home all summer, the thought of the air conditioners permanently breaking down presented Dain with a very uncomfortable situation.

Mr. Hall suggested that Dain seriously consider purchasing two new air conditioner units soon, or run the risk of these older air conditioner units breaking down in the middle of the summer when the daily heat temperature is near 110 degrees in Phoenix. Furthermore, replacing new units in the middle of the summer could take one to two weeks. Dain asked what the costs of these new units would be, and after quick calculation Mr. Hall confirmed that two new air conditioner units would cost Dain approximately $10,000. However, Mr. Hall made it clear that his air conditioning company has the best rates in the city, and he just replaced two of Dain's neighbors' air conditioner units as well. So if Dain needed a reference, he could simply check with his two neighbors.

Dain asked what the process was to order new air conditioners, and Mr. Hall confirmed that a down payment of $5,000 (or half the cost) was needed to secure his services, process the order, and schedule the installment. The entire process would take approximately two weeks. There was good news and bad news for Dain. The good news was he was about to receive a bonus of $7,500 from his job. The bad news was that Dain was not set to receive that bonus for another week. "I am sorry Mr. Hall. I just don't have $5,000 today," Dain said. While Mr. Hall clearly wanted the sale and was disappointed, he thanked Dain, left his business card, and said to give him a call if anything changes. The next day Dain called two of Mr. Hall's competitors because he wanted to shop for better pricing. However, both competitors were slightly higher priced than Mr. Hall's company, but the second competitor, named Bob's Air Conditioner, asked him, "Dain, I have a question for you. You said that your air conditioners are very old and that they are likely to break down permanently any time soon. And that you are currently in the market for new air conditioners before the summer temperatures hit 100-plus degrees. I know you said my price is $300 higher than Mr. Hall's company, but may I ask what is holding you back from making a decision today? Is there something specific holding you back that you are comfortable sharing?" Dain said, "Yes, I want to make a decision today so I can get the process moving forward, but I do not have the $5,000 today. I have to wait until my bonus comes next week before I can commit $5,000." Bob thanked him for sharing this information and said, "Dain, if all that is holding you up is a bonus coming next week, I could move forward today with the paperwork and ordering the units for you. I would simply need a down payment of $250 which is refundable if you change your mind. I don't mind waiting a week to secure the $5,000 down payment if it means earning your business and helping you move the process forward." Dain was convinced that no other company would let him move forward without a $5,000 down payment. He was pleasantly surprised that Bob's Air Conditioner company was flexible and reasonable, and despite being $300 more expensive than Mr. Hall's company he decided to sign the contract and get those air conditioners ordered. Bob earned the sale because he was skilled enough to uncover Dain's current objection and help him move toward his goal of replacing the air conditioner units before the summer arrived.

©Konstantin L/Shutterstock.com

Everybody in life will experience objection at some point. In professional selling, objections are not only anticipated—but should be planned for! That's right, shame on any professional sales representative who is caught off guard by a **sales objection**. A sales objection occurs when a prospect or existing customer either stalls or declines to purchase a service or product from a professional sales representative. In the above story of Dain and his aging air conditioners, Mr. Hall failed to uncover Dain's price objection. In fact, it was Bob's Air Conditioner company that landed the sale—despite being higher priced—because they took the time to find out WHAT was holding Dain back from making a final decision. Mr. Hall failed to uncover that Dain had the down payment, but needed just a few more business days to receive his bonus.

Sales Objection

when a prospect or existing customer either stalls or declines to purchase a service or product from a professional sales representative.

In this chapter we will discuss some of the reasons why prospects and customers object to purchasing a product or a service. Then we will discuss some of the most common objections that sales professionals experience. We will also discuss some of the skills and talking points needed for addressing, uncovering, and overcoming sales objections. If applied correctly, these skills can potentially assist you in job interviews, sales careers, your personal relationships, and more.

WHY PROSPECTS AND CUSTOMERS OBJECT

If you do a quick search on the web of why prospects and customers object to buying a product or a service you will find that there are scores of reasons: price, fear, too busy, "we already have it" misunderstanding, timing, lack of trust, "everything is fine as is," previously bad experiences, predispositions, and so on.

FOUR COMMON REASONS PEOPLE OBJECT TO PURCHASING A PRODUCT OR A SERVICE

1. Services.

From a customer perspective, purchasing a service can be a more difficult process than a product because many customers cannot touch a service, nor can they "see" or "envision" what the service actually does for them. For example, if a landscaper knocked on a customer's door and offered to "take care" of their yard for $100 per month, there are customers who would not understand—or envision in their mind—exactly what it is this landscaper would do to earn the $100. Whereas, a product (computer, cell phone, etc.) is something a customer can touch, examine, and test. Another example of a service is an interior designer. Interior designers charge an hourly rate to come into your home and provide "ideas" on how to stage your furniture, colors to paint the walls, pictures to hang and where. Yet, some people may have a difficult time paying for such a service because they cannot see or envision the end result. Others who trust interior designers and appreciate their ability to transform the look and feel of a home will pay hundreds or even thousands of dollars for such a valuable service.

Here are two suggestions for helping prospects and customers overcome service objections: (1) Use visuals when possible. Using visuals will help prospects and customers see or envision the value of service. In fact, 3M Corporation states that visuals are processed by customers at a rate of 60,000 times faster than ordinary text (TeamWave CRM 2016). And (2) Deploy referrals and "word of mouth" marketing strategies when selling services. It's absolutely amazing how a strong "word of mouth" campaign/strategy can add to a professional sales representative's book of business. In fact, it is a safe bet that everyone reading this chapter right now has likely purchased something (product or service) because someone else "recommended" you to do so. For example, in Chandler, Arizona, there is a Facebook landing page called "Ocotillo Friends." The site has approximately 31,000 Facebook followers, and one of the primary purposes of the site is for local community members to "ask" the group for referrals on landscapers, lawyers, accountants, and advice on contractors and doctors. If one person asks for a recommendation for a reputable landscaper, it is not uncommon for fifteen to twenty local community members to make recommendations on who to call for landscaping. These community members turn to each other to find out who does good work, and who does not do good work. As a result, many contractors—who do a great job—ask to be "recommended" on Ocotillo Friends, Facebook page. This is a far more effective marketing and sales strategy than leaving a simple flyer in someone's door. Think about it like this: if you were in trouble and needed a lawyer, are you more inclined to ask family and friends for advice on a good lawyer to call? Or would you call the phone number of a lawyer found on a billboard?

2. Too Busy.

If you are in a professional sales capacity then you will undoubtedly make sales calls to prospects and customers who are very busy (especially B2B customers). Generally speaking, people do not like getting calls from sales professionals. Since most prospects and customers are busy they are likely to tell sales professionals "not now" or "call me next month" or "I am just heading into a meeting/appointment." Nonetheless, prospects and customers do have purchasing needs (especially in the B2B market).

So if they are genuinely too busy, here is one way to approach or overcome that objection: make an appointment. Consider this scenario:

SCENARIO 1: A medical sales representative calls the procurement department of a major hospital. The procurement director is definitely interested in this rep's products, but unfortunately today is a bad day and she is slammed with meetings at the hospital all day. So they tell the medical sales representative to call back in two weeks when things slow down. If the medical sales representative hangs up the phone and calls back in two weeks, the odds are very good that he/she will encounter the same phone call experience as they did the first time! "Call me in two weeks . . . I'm busy."

SCENARIO 2: A medical sales representative calls the procurement department of a major hospital. The procurement director is definitely interested in this rep's products, but unfortunately today is a bad day and she is slammed with meetings at the hospital all day. So they tell the medical sales representative to call back in two weeks when things slow down.

Except THIS time the medical sales representative says, "Thanks Sheila, I know you are super busy and that you have things coming at you from every angle. Is there a recommended day that is better to connect up with you than others?"

To this the procurement director says, "Uhhhhh, sure. Tuesday's are better for me." (*Now this part is where a true professional gains a commitment and lands the meeting.*)

The medical sales representative says, "Okay, Tuesday it is. Is there a time of day on Tuesdays that works best? Do you prefer early morning before the rush? Or later in the day when things quiet down?"

Procurement director says, "I'd rather you call first thing in the morning. I get here at 8, but once 9 a.m. hits I am pulled into all kinds of meetings and situations."

The medical sales representative says, "Okay, great. How about we shoot for Tuesday the 24th at 8:15 a.m. This will give you a few minutes to get in, get situated, and then I will give you a call. Will that work for you?"

Procurement director responds, "It should work just fine."

The medical sales representative says, "Great, I will send you a calendar invite so it's on your calendar. We'll keep the meeting to no more than 25–30 minutes because I know you have a lot going on at 9 a.m. And . . . I am certain you will see tremendous value in our conversation. Plus, it will be great to connect up!"

Procurement director responds, "Okay, sounds good. Thanks." Call ends.

Which scenario do you prefer? When prospects and customers are busy—and many of them are—it is recommended to get on their calendar so you can have their full attention. This same principle also applies to hiring managers and job interviews. The goal is to get in front of the hiring manager and get the job.

3. *New Task Purchasing.*

When prospects and customers are buying something that they have purchased regularly in the past—such as light bulbs for the office, ink or paper for the printer, or renewing licensing/access for particular software, the decision to purchase is relatively an easy one. This is an easier decision for the buyer because they are simply ordering more of what they are already comfortable with (and have low risk of making a mistake). However, if a professional sales representative is selling (or recommending) a product or service that is new (i.e., a caravan versus an SUV; or a new telecommunication technology versus the ordinary office phones that have been used for years) these situations will generally evoke buyer objections. Not only is this new product or service a deviation from the norm, it is also a "risk" for the buyer or purchasing manager because this purchase may cause disruption with others in the office.

In these circumstances—when you are selling something NEW to a prospect or customer—here are three recommendations that could potentially help you overcome objections and ultimately earn the sale: First, be in a position to provide detailed facts and information. Remember, this is a deviation from their previous buying pattern, so there is a chance they will become uncomfortable with the new inner workings and results of this new product or service. Therefore, it is recommended to talk slow and walk them through the details of how this product or service not only works, but also the impact it will have on their performance, and the cost associated with making the purchase. Speaking too quickly may unintentionally send the message to the buyer that you are trying to hide details or intimidate the buyer. Lastly, after you walked them through the details, take the time to ask if there is anything they would like explained again. Second, when a prospect or customer is purchasing something new or deviating from a former buying pattern, it may be wise to ask the customer who else is part of the decision-making process. For example, if this is an expensive product or service—such as a $250,000 ultrasound machine for a hospital—the Chief Financial Officer (CFO) may be a significant "influencer" in that decision. If this is the case, it is better to know this information upfront and, if possible, invite the CFO to the meeting or call. In fact, expect that the CFO will weigh in, and either be prepared to meet them—or—provide the prospect with enough financial details so he/she can articulate the facts to the CFO.

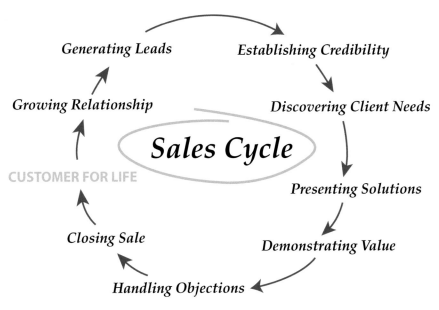

© Kendall Hunt Publishing Company

Third, in New Task Buying/Purchasing situations we recommend you develop a "why behind the what" mentality. Too often sales professionals do a fantastic job of explaining WHAT the product/service is, but a lousy job of articulating WHY this provides value. Remember when it comes to services the buyer can see what you are saying, but not always WHY it benefits his/her company. Consider talking points such as: Here is what the product does, and here are two ways how it could help your front office. Imagine a pool cleaner saying to you, "We would clean the pool every week and take care of all the chemicals. This will save you more time to spend with your family, and you would not waste time driving to the pool store to buy chemicals every week." Or imagine a software sales representative saying, "The software has a 'paid time off feature (PTO)' feature that allows PTO requests to shoot directly to the department manager's computer, cell phone, and/or tablet. This way, if the manager is traveling, has the day off, or in meetings, he/she can see in real time NOT only the PTO request, but what other employees have already taken off that day. Now managers can assure the assembly line is adequately staffed at all times!"

4. *You don't know what you don't know.*

There are many instances in which a buyer or prospect will object—not because they don't want the product or service—but rather because their business is functioning JUST fine at this time, and they are not aware of a whole new way of approaching a business model. For example, perhaps a small manufacturing office has historically used the United States Postal Service (USPS) for all of their mail and package shipping needs. Let's assume most of their clients live either within city limits or within twenty miles of the city. Imagine a day when the office manager receives a sales call from a sales representative at UberABC company attempting to sell "UberABC Delivery" as a new service that is taking the city by storm. Some of the highlighted benefits of these new services would include:

- ✓ Door-to-door service

- ✓ Same day delivery (probably even same hour delivery, depending on where the package is going in the city)

- ✓ Cheaper costs

- ✓ Business partners and customers who are happier with quicker turn-around time

Receiving a customer objection on a sales call like UberABC Delivery should be expected, anticipated, and prepared for because the office manager will likely have a tough time envisioning how this service will replace the USPS and improve customer relations. In these "new task" selling circumstances it is recommended to land an appointment and <u>have the meeting in person</u>.

Again, not only is the product or service new . . . the concept of UberABC Delivery is potentially frightening from a variety of perspectives:

- ✓ Trust—can we trust these random drivers/people to deliver our critically important packages?

- ✓ Fear—will our insurance even cover this delivery method? What will our clients think?

- ✓ Can't see or envision it—what are we getting ourselves into?

- ✓ What will my boss say to this change?

In these circumstances, it is also recommended that the sales representative **Parallel the Client**: process in which the sales representative uses specific product/service examples from either the client's competitors or client's industry to illustrate that the newly suggested product/service is trustworthy and deserving of further consideration.

One last comment on "You don't know what you don't know": one of the largest construction rental companies in the world told a story about a study they performed. It is actually quite fascinating. The company noticed that when a buyer had a choice between their construction rental equipment company vs. all the other competitors, they (construction rental company) won/landed the sale nearly 75 percent of the time. However, in this research they found a staggering statistic that only 40 percent of the market was "seeking" to buy construction rental equipment. So for the customers that WERE looking, this was great news for the large rental company. Nonetheless, it begged the question: where is the remaining 60 percent of the market? Their research found that 60 percent of the market was defaulting to their current buying status and not looking for a new construction rental company. In other words, 60 percent of the market wasn't looking for a new partner. The client did not know they necessarily needed to make a change. So the Chief Sales Officer decided to develop a strategy to proactively go out and target the 60 percent of the market. Moral of the story is: many clients don't know what they don't know— you have to go on the offense and take your message TO THEM!

> ### *Parallel the Client*
> process in which the sales representative uses specific product/service examples from either the client's competitors or client's industry to illustrate that the newly suggested product/service is trustworthy and deserving of further consideration.

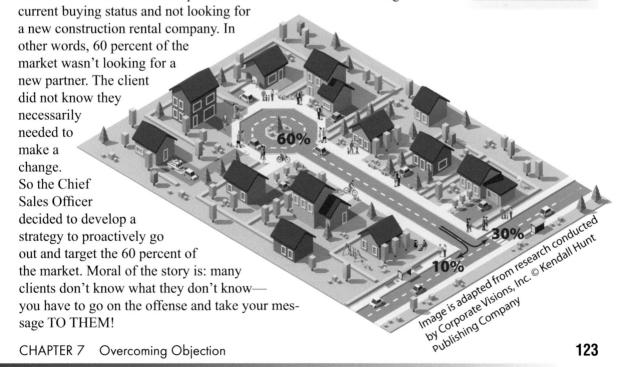

Image is adapted from research conducted by Corporate Visions, Inc. © Kendall Hunt Publishing Company

These are just a few of the explanations and reasons that people object. As we said earlier, there is a wide variety of reasons that people will either stall or decline from purchasing with you. Now let's take a look at some types of objections that are particularly common in the professional selling world.

Price Objection

occurs when a buyer either stalls or declines to purchase a product/service due to the cost directly associated with that product/ service.

The most common objection is price objection, and just about every one of us has declined to buy a product or service due to price. **Price objection** occurs when a buyer either stalls or declines to purchase a product/service due to the cost directly associated with that product/service. Professional sales representatives should not only expect and anticipate price objections, but be prepared to uncover the reasoning that price is the objection. For example, as we discussed earlier, perhaps they do not have the money to make a purchase today but they will receive a yearly bonus in one month. Or, perhaps they do not have the financial means to pay $3,000 for a new couch, but they do have the financial means to pay $250 for 12 months at 0% interest.

The secret to overcoming a customer's price objection is to UNCOVER what the objection is in the first place. Here are two ways to approach a buyer who is demonstrating price objection (**empathize** about their objection **first**, and then **uncover** their true objection **second**):

1. "I understand $3,000 is a lot of money, especially with the holidays coming. Can you help me understand why it is that now might be a more difficult time to make the purchase versus a few months ago, or in a few months?"

2. "I can totally empathize that resealing the doors and windows throughout the main floor of your house would not be a cheap endeavor. But if there was a hole in the side of your house the size of a basketball, wouldn't you be inclined to fix it and stop these high energy bills once and for all? Because all of these leaks in the windows and doors add up to a hole in your house the size of a basketball."

The customer's initial shock is the price, but as you can see in the second scenario sometimes a professional sales representative can overcome the objection by helping the customer see "the bigger picture."

Time objection is another common objection that professional sales representatives will experience. **Time objection** occurs when a buyer either stalls or declines to purchase a product/service due to the timing of the sales pitch. While price objection is the most common, timing can be a tactic used by the buyer either intentionally or unintentionally. For example, the customer might be interested in making the purchase, but simply needs time to think about it and do their due diligence. Others may want to make the purchase, but the time of year is a factor for reasons such as impact to their business (very common with insurance sales because policy renewal is usually semi-annual or annual). Hiring managers often use time objection to allow more time for interviewing other candidates and adhering to their company's hiring "process."

> ### *Time Objection*
>
> occurs when a buyer either stalls or declines to purchase a product/service due to the timing of the sales pitch.

TWO SUGGESTED METHODS OF ADDRESSING A TIMING OBJECTION

1. "I understand that you need a couple weeks to think about it. It is a big decision. Do you mind if I simply check in with you next week, not to rush you, but to pop my head in the door to see if any new questions or concerns arrived?"

2. "I understand now is a bad time. But may I ask what your timeline is for making a decision so that I can touch base with you at a later date and keep the conversation going with you?"

Notice how in scenario 1 a couple things happen: (1) the seller is allowing the buyer his/her requested time to make a decision. The sales professional is not rushing the process; however, (2) the sales representative is asking a non-threatening question about simply "checking in" to see if there are any concerns or new questions. This approach makes it harder for the buyer to say no, and generates a higher probability for the sales professional to stay in front of the customer while keeping the conversation alive. According to the marketing research firm, Marketing Donut, 44 percent of sales professionals walk away after the first "no" (or objection) (Clay, n.d.). And another 22 percent give up after the second "no" (or objection). This means most sales professionals do not effectively uncover the objection, nor do they seek opportunities to check back in with the customer at the appropriate time. Keeping in front of the client is critical to succeeding in professional selling.

©iQoncept/Shutterstock.com

Need Objection

occurs when a buyer either stalls or declines to purchase a product/service because the status quo of the buyer's needs appears sufficient.

Need objection is another common objection that sales professionals will experience. **Need objection** occurs when a buyer either stalls or declines to purchase a product/service because the status quo of the buyer's needs appears sufficient. Of course, there are times when buyers have a process, procedure, product, or level of service that is working just fine. But many times buyers are not always aware that they have a need. The secret to uncovering need objections is to first ask the customer these two questions: (1) what is their favorite part about the product/service, and (2) what is their greatest frustration about their current product or service.

When a customer believes that he/she has everything they need—and therefore object to your product/service—the recommended solution to uncovering and overcoming the objection is to differentiate by service. Once the sales professional discovers what the customers like about the product/service and what it is they would like to see improved about the product/service, the sales professional has potentially opened a new window of opportunity to make the case for a sale.

Consider this scenario:

CUSTOMER: "No thanks Alex. My landscapers are doing just fine, so right now we won't need your services."

ALEX/SALES REP: "Oh I perfectly understand Mrs. Aughinbaugh. But may I ask, would you be comfortable sharing with me what is your favorite thing about your current landscapers? And maybe one thing that makes them imperfect? Something they could do slightly better?"

CUSTOMER: "Well, I have gone through five different landscapers in two years. And now I finally have someone who shows up on time and is consistent. As for what they could do better? Oh, I don't know. I wish they would not blow so much debris into my pool because it clogs it up at times."

ALEX/SALES REP: "Okay, that's good. And I can totally appreciate finding a landscaper that is consistent, affordable, and does good work. If my company could match their price, show up every week on time without fail, and we not only kept the debris out of your pool, but also took the extra steps of spraying for weeds in your driveway and sidewalk out front—would you be open to giving us a shot at your business?"

Many professional sales representatives would have accepted the customer's original needs objection statement ("I like my current landscapers. Not now please.") and simply walked away. But Alex asked one to two simple questions, and was able to get the customer to admit that there is room for improvement—with customer service. Hence, the customer did not originally think there was a need for a new landscaper, but she now has a potentially better offer on the table at no additional cost to her. Everybody wins.

ETHICAL DILEMMA

Emma Dietrich has been with WhatAPrice Cars for six months. The WhatAPrice Car dealership was known for aggressive pricing and negotiating, and also for sales professionals who worked solely on a commission basis. Joe Russo was in the market for a used BMW, and he had a budget of $40,000. He came in on the last day of the month because he heard that WhatAPrice Cars has monthly quotas that often lead to smoking hot deals for the buyer.

©Phat1978/Shutterstock.com

After two hours of discussions and test drives, Mr. Russo was 90 percent certain about the car he wanted, and they began negotiating on the price for a 2016 BMW. "Mr. Russo, the best we can do is $40,800, and that's only because today is the last day of the month. If we do not agree on a deal right now, then either someone else may buy that car or the price could change since tomorrow is the start of a new month. What do you think?" Emma said with confidence. Mr. Russo was slightly uncomfortable because $40,000 was his original budget, but he sure loved this car. "I don't know, Emma," he said, "I promised myself $40,000 was the most I would spend, and while an additional $800 isn't a deal breaker I may need to think about this over-night." Emma's training taught her that if a customer walks off the car lot the probability of the customer coming back and buying a car significantly declines. Emma also knew that if he came back tomorrow and made an offer that WhatAPrice Car may still offer that same deal, but she cannot guaran-tee it since the dealership incentives may change. What should Emma do?

1. Stick to her training, keep him at the negotiating table, and find out what exactly is giving Mr. Russo pause? If so, what questions would be appropriate for Mr. Russo?

2. Tell him to take a night and sleep on it (knowing there is high probability he may not return), but ask if it is okay that she gives him a call first thing tomorrow morning?

3. Give up some of her commission to sweeten the pot and help make the deal go through today? This is very common in car sales. Some commission is better than no commission.

Product objections are fairly common in professional selling, especially when a product has new features or invokes new emotions from the buyer. **Product objection** occurs when a buyer either stalls or declines to purchase a product due to the product's physical attributes or the negative emotions it may invoke. One example of potential product objection could be the Toyota Prius and the benefits of its hybrid battery, low CO_2 emissions, and miles per gallon. However, as impressive as these benefits are to the eco-friendly consumer, the sight of a smaller, compact car may offset the tremendous benefits of the miles per gallon and low CO_2 emissions. While a similar argument can be made about any car, make, or model, the point is that there are consumers who may decline to purchase a Toyota Prius solely on the appearance of the car or the negative feelings it may invoke (from being small, too eco-friendly, peer pressure).

When a customer stalls or objects based off a product's physical attributes or the negative emotions associated with the product, potential solutions to uncovering and overcoming the objection will be determined by the questions you ask, and then how you redirect their attention to what their goals of purchasing were in the first place. Consider this scenario:

CUSTOMER: "I just cannot see myself driving a Prius. It's small, and people may laugh at me. My friends are used to seeing me drive a Toyota 4runner."

SALES PROFESSIONAL: "Help me understand why people would laugh at you? When you came in today, you said your goal was to purchase a car that was safe, cheap on gas, eco-friendly on the environment, and affordable. If each of these four goals are met, wouldn't you be the one laughing every time you fill up at the pump?"

Notice here how the sales professional used effective questioning to discover the three to four most important features and benefits about purchasing a new car, and then masterfully reminded the customer of the reasoning he/she came in to purchase a vehicle in the first place: your goal was to buy a car that was safe, cheap on gas, eco-friendly, and affordable. Why would people laugh at you for a driving a car that helps you meet your personal and professional goals?

CHAPTER SUMMARY

In this chapter we discussed that there are countless reasons and explanations as to why customers object to buying. Sales objections occur when a customer either stalls or declines to make a purchase. Some of the more common reasons why people object are: services (I can't touch it), I'm too busy (call me in a week), it's new (adventure into the unknown), or the customer simply doesn't know that they have a need (everything is working just fine right now). For customers who object due to the intangibilities of

> ### *Product Objection*
>
> occurs when a buyer either stalls or declines to purchase a product due to the product's physical attributes or the negative emotions it may invoke.

services, showing a visual to the buyer may prove helpful. For a customer who says they are too busy, it is recommended to make an appointment with the customer. If a customer objects due to the fact that the product/service is new, remember that having lots of information and facts on hand will provide credibility when speaking with the buyer. And lastly, there are buyers who do not know how to process the information of your new product or service, mainly because they have never heard of it before. We used the example of UberABC Delivery as a solution to replace the United States Postal Service. If a customer has never heard about UberABC Delivery services, they may be inclined to object to purchasing this service from you. In these situations, it is recommended to meet the client in person to not only build rapport and credibility, but also to show a visual or "demo" for how this new service can/will benefit their company.

There are four objections that are particularly common to the sales profession: (1) price objection, (2) time objection, (3) need objection, and (4) product objection. The most common of these four is price objection because most consumers have either stalled or declined to purchase a product or service due to price. Sometimes the customer is awaiting a bonus, income tax return, or inheritance, so taking the time to uncover why price is an obstacle may elicit that price is not an obstacle after all. Time objection is another very common objection in business. In these circumstances the secret is to remain persistent without being pushy. It's acceptable to ask the customer if you may check in with him/her in a timely fashion (remaining "top of mind" and in front of the client). Need objection occurs when customers fundamentally believe that their system or process is currently working just fine, and therefore no change is needed at this time. For these customers, consider making "customer service" your differentiator. And lastly, product objection occurs when a product's physical appearance or negative emotions are the root causes for the customer stalling or declining a purchase. In these circumstances, it is recommended to identify the buyer's primary goals before suggesting products to purchase. This way, you can keep the customer focused on the important things, and you will be able to articulate why they came in to make a purchase in the first place.

REFERENCES

Clay, Robert. (n.d.) "Why you must follow up leads." Marketing Donut. http://www.marketingdonut.co.uk/sales/sales-techniques-and-negotiations/why-you-must-follow-up-leads

TeamWave CRM. April 8, 2016. 50 Amazing Sales Prospecting Stats That Will Improve The Way You Sale (slide 39). https://blog.teamwave.com/2016/04/08/50-amazing-sales-prospecting-stats-that-will-make-you-a-sales-rock-star/

7

HOMEWORK

Sean Smith is a sales associate for Dietrich Pest Control in Phoenix, Arizona. Arizona has a heavy population of spiders and scorpions. Pest control is a highly desired service in the Phoenix market. His job entails door-to-door selling. Nonetheless, Sean has been successful over the past two years and has earned 20 percent market share in the five subdivisions he targets. Additionally, about once every month Sean receives an unsolicited referral from a current customer.

On this particular day Sean was greeted at the front door by a homeowner named Jay Totolo. After two to three minutes of discussing the possibilities of Dietrich's Pest Control as a monthly service, Jay began to show signs of indecision and discomfort.

SEAN: "So you currently do not have a pest control company that you work with?"

JAY: "No. I spray the yard myself when I have time."

SEAN: "How does that process of managing your pest control yourself work for you and your home? Do you find it easy to do? Cheaper? Effective with your pest control?"

JAY: "I do the best I can, but obviously I am not an expert. It runs me about $40 per month purchasing the materials and spray, and it takes me about two hours over a weekend to get it done."

SEAN: "Would you be open to giving us a shot?"

JAY: "I don't know, Sean. You seem like a nice guy. And I see Dietrich Pest Control signs throughout the community. But I'm just not sure right now if I want to hire a Pest Control service."

QUESTION 1: What questions can Sean ask that would potentially help Jay overcome his concerns?

QUESTION 2: Sean has earned 20 percent market share in nearby developments. Is there something specific Sean can do with this factual information to help Jay make a decision?

CHAPTER 8
Positioning

Victorious warriors win first and then go to war,
while defeated warriors go to war first and then seek to win.

— *Sun Tzu*

©Yuganov Konstantin/Shutterstock.com

CHAPTER OBJECTIVES

✓ Define the meaning of sales positioning

✓ Discuss the importance and purpose of positioning as a critical tactic leveraged at every level of the sales life cycle

✓ Examine five new positioning techniques that could improve relationships with prospects, clients, and your business network

In 2016, Randy Tranger, a women's healthcare representative from ATD, was driving through town and decided to make an impromptu stop at Sanford Hospital to say hello to his client who was the Director of Procurement, Mike Earle. Three months earlier Randy sold two ultrasound machines to Mike, and each machine cost the hospital approximately $250,000. It was a good sale, yielding Randy a commission check for $20,000. It was safe to say that Sanford Hospital and Mike Earle were a good client!

Randy did not have an appointment, and he knew that Mike would likely not purchase any additional ultrasound machines for the coming year. Nonetheless, he was passing through town and this would be an opportune time to say hello to a good client, get some face time with his client, and to see how Mike was liking the two ultrasound machines. After exchanging pleasantries, Randy apologized for the impromptu visit and reiterated that he would not stay long. "Don't be crazy, Randy. Sit down. How have you been?" Mike replied. The two sat down and Randy said, "I know you just purchased a couple machines with us, and that you won't be buying additional machines for a while. But may I ask, how are the two new machines working for you? Any problems or concerns?" Mike opened his eyes wide and said, "No way, the machines are fantastic and the doctors love them. Other than my boss bickering about their price, everybody seems to be pleased. But Randy, I'm actually glad you stopped by. There's something we need to discuss, but we cannot talk here. Are you available for dinner tonight?" Randy's next appointment was not until the following morning, so he quickly agreed to meet Mike at 5:30 p.m.

That evening Mike got right to the point, "Thank you so much for meeting me. What a day. What a week. Things have gotten crazy around here, and my head is spinning." Randy interpreted Mike's upbeat tempo and body language as seemingly good news, but he wisely remained in listening mode as Mike clearly had some big news to discuss. And so Mike continued, "Okay, so here's why I wanted to meet you after work. As you know, we are happy with the machines you sold us. The doctors and nurses are also happy, and there has not been any issues or problems. However, we just got word that we are building a new hospital—construction starting this year. The new hospital will be right here in this city, and it will be three times the size of our current hospital. As you know I am head of procurement, so I will be busy making all of the new equipment purchases for the new hospital. But Randy, here's my challenge: My boss thinks ATD has good products, great technology, but that you guys are way too expensive. We are estimating that I will need to purchase six to eight ultrasound machines next year, but this time he wants me to bid it out."

Randy processed the magnitude of the order and almost fell off his chair. With a sale like this not only would he see a huge commission check, but Randy would no doubt be the front-runner for top salesman in his company. "Mike, this is fantastic news. I'm happy for you, the hospital, and the community. No matter how you look at this, it's a great opportunity. You said that you are happy with the machines, the technology, and our service. What can I do to convince your boss to stick with ATD, and of course me. Should I give him a call and talk to him?" Mike listened intently to Randy, and then said, "No. No. No. There's a couple moving parts here, and while price is something we need to address, there is a bigger picture. Yes, we do need ATD to be competitive with its pricing. Nobody says you have to be the cheapest, but we do need to be competitive. But again, it's more than that. This decision to buy the machines is not going to happen in the next eight to ten months. The hospital's administration is highly encouraging employee and community engagement in the development of this new facility. Therefore, we are having bi-monthly meetings with staff and members of the community to get input and public buy-in. The doctors will be present at these meetings. Why don't you plan on attending these meetings and making sure the doctors and nurses know who you are? I recommend you reiterate that You and ATD have been long-time partners of Sanford. My boss will also be at these meetings, so you will have many opportunities to engage him—*in person*—as well. Between myself, the doctors and nurses, the patients, and my boss, you may be able to position yourself and ATD as an indispensable strategic partner." Randy agreed that landing this sale would take more effort than usual. He would need to position himself well with a variety of staff and administration. During the next eight months, if he did position himself well, it could make it more difficult on the hospital's administration to buy from an ATD competitor.

Randy made it a point to attend every meeting, shake every hand, and answer every question. Mike was right, the doctors and nurses also attended every meeting, and they often had questions for Randy. While Mike's boss did not attend every meeting, he was present at a few. Each time he saw Randy he had questions about competing hospitals, various machines that they purchase, and what new technology ATD was working on. He even inquired about ATD's ability to consider "customized orders" that could potentially allow some ultrasound machines to provide full-service capabilities and services while other machines offer fewer—but more common—capabilities and services. Having advanced technology was critical in a hospital, but sometimes the full depth and breadth of the technology is not required for common patient visits.

Randy began to work with ATD's operations department on the concept of customized orders, and within five months ATD not only agreed to offer customized options with ultrasound machines, but free training to all relevant staff during that first thirty days of the purchase. And that was not all. On the hospital's administrative side, Mike's boss worked with Sanford's billing department and was able to conclude that the patients' billing rates could potentially be lowered if the doctors decided to use the more advanced machinery only when necessary for the patient. During the course of nine months, Randy was able to position himself strategically—one meeting at a time—with doctors and nurses, members of the hospital's procurement department, and of course with Mike's boss. When the decision came to purchase ultrasound machines, Mike and his boss were in full support of purchasing all new ultrasound machines through ATD and Randy. Not only was ATD and its technology a good fit for the hospital's business plan and patient experience, but Randy was an indispensable business partner who was willing to spend the time and resources necessary to understand his clients and ensure their success.

POSITIONING

In the first seven chapters we covered a variety of ways to improve your selling techniques and significantly improve your selling position with prospects and clients. Now we will take a closer look at the meaning of positioning, how it could impact your relationship building, and discuss five new ways for you to implement positioning techniques into your selling routine.

In professional selling, the art of "positioning" is arguably the most important skill set to develop, because positioning with clients occurs at every phase of the sales life cycle. For example, in Chapter 1 we discussed the concepts of trust and relatability as well as a variety of practical methods for you to implement into your daily behaviors. By improving your trustworthiness and relatability with other people, *you are positioning yourself* to be a

©Monster Ztudio/Shutterstock.com

more successful sales professional. If customers do not trust you, or cannot relate to you, then you will not be well positioned to develop a relationship with them. In Chapter 4 we discussed the concept of networking, and once again demonstrated a variety of practical ways and means that you could apply these tactics into your daily routine. By networking effectively, *you are positioning yourself* to develop those relationships. Therefore, **sales positioning** is a process in which the sales professional takes proactive steps—at every stage in the sales life cycle—to improve his/her practical selling techniques and/or behaviors for the purpose of continuously improving his/her position or standing with prospects, clients, or business network.

The story about Randy and Mike drives home the concept that sales positioning takes place at every level of the sales life cycle. For example, there was a time and place that Randy and Mike did not know each other, but the business community brought them together: Mike has a need (purchases hospital equipment) and Randy has a solution (sells ultrasound machines). At some point, Randy had to earn the trust of Mike and *position* himself to propose new equipment orders. Randy's company, ATD, also played a significant role in positioning with Mike and the hospital because the ATD equipment needs to be delivered on time, function properly, and provide value to the doctors, nurses, and patients at the hospital. And lastly, Randy was faced with a choice: stop in to say an impromptu hello to a client—or—drive on by and head toward the next city. Randy made the correct decision to stop by and see the client. Not only did this position himself well with

Sales Positioning

a process in which the sales professional takes proactive steps—at every stage in the sales life cycle—to improve his/her practical selling techniques and/or behaviors for the purpose of continuously improving his/her position or standing with prospects, clients, or business network.

Mike (learning about the new hospital and his boss's desire to bid out future ultrasound machines), but it also positioned Randy to *continue* staying in front of the hospital administration team and ultimately avoid the bidding war with his competitors.

FIVE SPECIFIC TECHNIQUES TO IMPROVE YOUR POSITION WITH PROSPECTS AND CLIENTS

1. *It is human nature to learn by repetition.*

As we discussed at the onset of Chapter 1, success in professional selling is not the result of doing one specific thing really good, but rather a wide variety of techniques and behaviors—all done very well. Hence, the concept of *7 Ways 7 Times.* One of the recommended techniques to positioning with a prospect or a customer is to make sure that they hear your sales message through a variety of thoughtful and appropriate methods: verbally in person, through e-mails, texting, phone calls, marketing materials, social media, video chat, and so on. This is NOT to suggest bombarding customers with sales calls and too much information. As we discussed in Chapter 6, it is recommended to touch base with a customer at least five times per year, and depending on the customer . . . sometimes more.

The reasoning behind messaging through repetition is because many customers (just like us) are busy, have many other responsibilities, and can be easily distracted. Therefore, we recommend you improve your positioning with clients by a strategic—well thought out—campaign of touch points during the sales cycle. Although your conversations may vary, the essence of your message to the client should remain consistent. What you say, how you say it, when you say it, the vehicle you deliver the message, etc., are all designed to keep your customers focused on you and the product/service. Consider these two scenarios:

A. Bob is a professional sales representative for Xerox. At a conference in February he met the COO of a parts manufacturer from Chicago. Over coffee, the COO confided to Bob that his company would be purchasing ten new copy/printer machines in November. At the end of the conference Bob exchanged contact information with the COO, and promised he would be in touch about a proposal for the copy/printers. After returning home from the conference Bob became busy, and while he made a mental note about the COO, he did not touch base or make contact for eight months. In October Bob gave the COO a call about the copy/printers he mentioned in

February, and inquired about an opportunity to bid. Upon answering the phone and listening to Bob's comments, the COO paused and replied, "I'm sorry, this is Bob who?"

B. Charles is a professional sales representative for Xerox. At a conference in February he met the COO of a parts manufacturer from Chicago. Over coffee, the COO confided to Charles that his company would be purchasing ten new copy/printer machines in November. At the end of the conference Charles exchanged contact information with the COO, and promised he would be in touch about a proposal for the copy/printers. After returning home from the conference Charles sent the COO an e-mail thanking him for his time at the conference. Charles informed the COO that in July his company would be rolling out the new Copy/Printer 6000 Series that would have 25 percent more printing speed and 75 percent more memory for large printing and scanning needs. He promised to send the COO some additional information on the new machines once his marketing department had the opportunity to put the materials together. Sure enough, in June Charles sent the COO additional marketing materials, as well as some financing and leasing options, and said he was excited to compete for the ten new machines in October. Charles also successfully connected with the COO by LinkedIn.

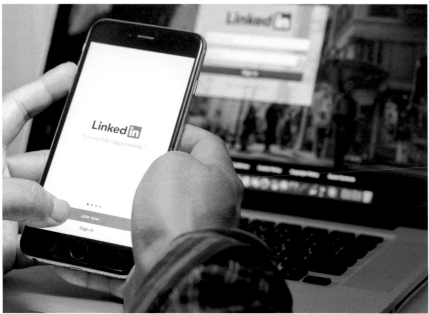

Larger audiences—especially in public speaking settings when speeches are lengthy—learning by repetition also applies. But the challenge becomes holding their attention long enough to be repetitive. When communicating with a larger audience (three or more) it becomes increasingly difficult for the professional sales representative to adequately hold everyone's attention. This is largely due to the larger audience believing that you are not staring at THEM. In other words, "it is okay to check your cell phone quickly . . . because she is not looking at ME right now." In these situations it is recommended to simplify your message (the larger the audience, the simpler the conversation) and hold their attention by keeping the conversation interesting and engaging. For example, ask for a show of hands for how many people have heard of your company. Engagement will help a large audience's attention.

2. _Know the political landscape._

A smart technique for a sales professional is to seek political counseling. **Political counseling** occurs when a client is willing to provide a sales professional with the political landscape taking place inside the customer's business. Consider the story at the beginning of the chapter with Randy and Mike. If the doctors and nurses were the end-users of the ultrasound machines, then it is conceivable that several doctors and/or nurses have the ability to undermine ATD and Randy by recommending a competitor's product. However, if Mike is willing to provide Randy access to the doctors and nurses (and perhaps some intel on what they are saying behind the scenes), Randy can position himself to address their concerns, provide additional customer service, and build rapport with the staff. However, political counseling would not be possible if Randy was not well positioned and trusted by Mike in the first place. Hence, _positioning_ is a continuous process and occurs at every level of the sales process.

> ### Political Counseling
> occurs when a client is willing to provide a sales professional with the political landscape taking place inside the customer's business.

3. _Operational counseling._

Knowing the political landscape that impacts your customers is smart business. Equally important is **operational counseling** which refers to information provided to professional sales representatives concerning the relevant technical systems, business processes, and company policies in the customer's organization. Operational counseling is a very useful positioning technique because the sales professional can discover, for example, not only who the decision-maker is but also his/her influentials who are part of the decision-making process. If you are selling directly to the COO, but the pricing mandates that the CFO be involved in the buying process, then knowing this information _positions_ the sales professional to answer financial questions in a sales meeting (or, if the I.T. department is part of the decision-making process, then the sales professional can position his/herself to anticipate and answer the technical questions from the I.T. department). Can you imagine a scenario in which the sales professional was expecting to meet only the COO, and was NOT prepared to meet the CFO and I.T. Director at a sales meeting? Lack of positioning and planning (or Operational counseling) in this area could result in a disastrous meeting.

> ### Operational Counseling
> refers to information provided to professional sales representatives concerning the relevant technical systems, business processes, and company policies in the customer's organization.

4. _Be the thought leader._

Another technique sales professionals can use to improve their positioning with the clients (and the industry at large) is to become a thought leader, or the go-to person for product expertise, industry trends, and answers to difficult questions. A **thought leader** is an individual who is recognized as an

> ### Thought Leader
> an individual who is recognized as an authority in a specific discipline, product/service, or industry.

authority in a specific discipline, product/service, or industry. One example of thought leadership is "following" a business connection on LinkedIn. Each day, week, or month you may notice that there are people on LinkedIn who simply post (or repost) interesting articles or facts about their company, discipline, or product/service. If a banker posts (or reposts) an interesting article about 0% down home loans on LinkedIn, he/she is sending the signal that they are experts on 0% down home loans. It would not be a surprise if a business connection "messaged" the thought leader asking "what credit scores qualify for a 0% down home loan?" or "I am interested in a no-money down home loan, where can I get more information?"

Another platform to become a thought leader is blogging about your company, industry, or product/service. Anybody can blog. Most professional sales representatives have clients, family, friends, or people in their network who will read what they have to say in these blogs. As we indicated with LinkedIn, you can take information and facts that already exist about your industry, company, or product/service and repackage the information with YOUR spin on it. The fact is, by speaking to an audience of followers you are *positioning yourself* as an expert or authority on the topic. (Note: Thought Leadership signifies that you are communicating reputable information, facts, and trends about your industry, company, or product/service. It assumes you have done your research and can defend your position. If you have an employer, it is recommended you talk to your employer and get buy-in from the employer BEFORE launching the campaign.)

A young sales professional may incorrectly assess that their age or experience inhibits their ability to become a thought leader. The authors of this textbook recommend becoming a thought leader early in your career. Post reputable information on LinkedIn and other social media sites; start a blog that drives home the quality, efficiency, and impact of your product or services; contribute to a relevant newsletter; and, one day—when you are ready—seek to become the speaker or panelist at a relevant conference. Your clients (and competition) _will_ take notice, and they will see you as the go-to expert.

5. Remain _top of mind_ with existing clients.

Top of Mind Positioning

tactic used by sales professionals to remain *relevant* to the buyer(s).

One of the biggest mistakes sales professionals make is not remaining top of mind with their existing client base. **Top of mind positioning** is the tactic used by sales professionals to remain *relevant* to the buyer(s). Remaining relevant is a subtle—not overt—approach to positioning. Two examples of remaining relevant with a client are:

    A. Calling/e-mailing/texting a client asking if they are considering attending a selected conference, social event, etc. (You are not asking or suggesting that they buy anything from you, but you are putting them in a position to communicate with you. For example, think of Bob and Charles asking the COO if he is attending that same conference NEXT February.)

B. Send a yearly Christmas card or anniversary card. For example, if a banker provided a home loan for a client, there is no harm sending an anniversary card saying "congrats on one year" or "Wow, time flies. I hope everything is great for you and the family." (Again, do not ask for anything or imply they buy something. By remaining relevant you are also positioning yourself to be the first person they DO call if a product or service is needed.)

Banking is a very common industry in which an existing customer will have his/her checking account, debit card, and car loan with one bank, but obtain their home mortgage or car insurance from a completely different financial institution. Why would a customer not want to have all of their basic financial needs in one bank? It would be easier and more convenient. Of course, sometimes there are better rates with a competitor.

The authors of this book do not fault anybody for searching out the best deals for their families. But too often customers are encouraged to do their mortgage where either their realtor suggests (because many realtors like working with specific bankers) or at a financial institution that their friends or family suggest. A mortgage is a service. Customers tend to purchase services by word of mouth and referrals. The same applies to car insurance: customers will sometimes purchase insurance where their family or friends recommend, despite their local bank offering the same service.

Therefore, a recommended technique to stay well positioned with existing clients is to stay top of mind with them.

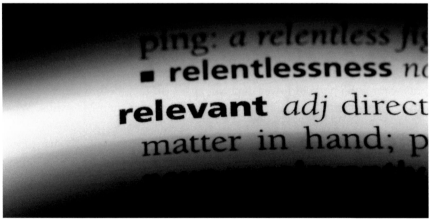

©Casimiro PT/Shutterstock.com

ETHICAL DILEMMA

Tim McCleary's Construction has been in business for fifteen years, and a common name in the Beachwood, New Jersey, community. Specializing in residential construction, owner Tim McCleary started out building just two to three houses per year, but after many years of excellent work, relationship building, and community involvement McCleary Construction was now building an average of twenty houses per year. Tim was bidding out plumbing work for his next five houses, and his policy was to get bids from at least three local plumbers. Billy Dietrich from Mr. Bill's Plumbing stopped by the office to drop off his bid and get some face time and rapport with the owner, Tim McCleary. "Mr. Bill, Thanks for stopping by. Are you dropping off your bid? Awesome. Sit down, let's grab a cup of coffee and talk," Tim said.

After a few pleasantries were exchanged, Mr. Bill asked if Tim received two other bids. Tim said, "Yep, my policy is to always get three. It's the only way I can ensure fair pricing, and another way for me to keep the costs down for my customers." Upon reviewing Mr. Bill's bid, Tim noticed that Mr. Bill was $28,000 cheaper than one bid, and $30,000 cheaper than the other bid. Furthermore, Mr. Bill was offering extended warranties on all plumbing—at no additional charge. Normally, Mr. Bill did not concern himself all that much with other contractors or what they charged. He always tried to keep his prices fair and earn his client's trust through old-fashioned customer service. "Tim, I don't know what the other guys are offering, but do I have a shot? I have been working with you for almost ten years, and I would like to retain my relationship with you and McCleary Construction." Tim smiled and said, "You do great work Bill. Always have. But I gotta tell you, the other two bids are 5 percent lower than yours. Your service is better than theirs, but price is a factor for me and my customers. If you could go another 5 percent lower and simply match theirs, we have a deal." Mr. Bill did quick math and decided to lower his price and take the deal. Tim stood up and asked Bill if he would like some coffee, and then asked to be excused for a minute. Upon Tim leaving the room Mr. Bill could not help but to notice the two competitors' bids laying on Tim's desk. Both bids were not 5 percent lower than Mr. Bill's. In fact, both were exceptionally higher—with the nearest one at $28,000 higher than Mr. Bill's. What should Mr. Bill do?

A. Be quiet, take the deal, and don't ruin a ten-year relationship?

B. Confront Tim when he gets back, and demand to renegotiate the 5 percent discount?

C. He had no business reading two different documents sitting on a customer's desk, so accept the fact that Tim was not the only one who acted unethically?

D. Walk out. Tim lied.

CHAPTER SUMMARY

Sales positioning is one of the most critical skill sets to develop in a professional selling career because it is designed to improve your standing with the client. Positioning takes place at every stage of the sales cycle, *and is a continuous effort*. Customers are very busy with their personal and professional lives. Therefore, due to the countless distractions that affect our clients, we may need to deploy a strategy of repetition. In other words, it may take a series of conversations and follow-ups for the client to process the value of your product or service. As discussed at the beginning of the chapter, knowing the political and operational landscape of a company is an art not a science. Positioning yourself properly with the client may lead to a point in the relationship in which the client is willing to share with you the political and operational landscape of the company. As we have seen with the story of Randy and ATD, the deal may have been lost to the competition had Randy not continuously improved his position and relationship with Mike.

©Olivier Le Moal/Shutterstock.com

Thought leadership is a recommended sales technique to deploy in your professional selling career. Imagine sharing with your hiring manager during the interview process that one of your goals in the first year is to become a thought leader? It is not only impressive to set a thought leadership goal in a job interview, but a smart sales tactic that will improve your position with prospects and customers. Lastly, top of mind is a technique designed to keep relevant in the mind of a customer. When an existing customer at a bank originates their home loan at a competing financial institution, it is usually the result of a realtor, family member, friend, or competitor recommending the customer go somewhere else. "My sister got a great rate on her home loan, so I went to her banker." Top of mind technique will improve your position with prospects and customers. Remember, this sales technique is subtle—not overt.

REFERENCES

Dumaine, Brian. 2014. "The Kings of Concentration." *Inc.* (May). https://www.inc.com/magazine/201405/brian-dumaine/how-leaders-focus-with-distractions.html

Journal of Media Education. January 2016. http://en.calameo.com/read/00009178915b8f5b352ba

Mark, Gloria. 2006. "Too Many Interruptions at Work?" Business Journal, June 8. Gallup News. http://news.gallup.com/businessjournal/23146/Too-Many-Interruptions-Work.aspx

8 HOMEWORK

Patti-Ann received a life-changing call from corporate: she will be moving from Minneapolis to Phoenix to open a new office for Rockaway Construction. During the past twenty years Rockaway Construction grew from 10 employees to 200, with revenues exceeding $300 million annually. From 2010–2017 Rockaway Construction was responsible for much of the K–12 new construction in Minneapolis, and had become internationally famous for building the new downtown Arts Center Building. Company leadership decided Phoenix was a market they could compete and thrive in, and all they needed was a special person to open the Phoenix office and make immediate inroads and connections with the community.

Patti-Ann's universal people skills and ability to network caught the eye of Chief Operation Officer John Hayden. Always expressing interest in making a move out of Minneapolis to warmer weather, Patti-Ann was happy to accept a job transfer down to Phoenix, Arizona.

Upon arriving in Phoenix two things caught Patti-Ann's attention: (1) most people in the Phoenix market have not heard of Rockaway Construction, and (2) the company lacked deep-rooted community relationships which were so helpful and instrumental with the growth in the Minneapolis market. Strong community relationships leads to establishing credibility with the business community, receiving insights on upcoming construction projects, and opportunities to position "early" in the decision-making process—particularly for school projects. She realized that it was HER JOB to help the company overcome these hurdles.

QUESTION 1: Go to www.valleypartnership.org and recommend two ways that Patti-Ann can help her company establish itself in the market and position for projects with potential clients. Please defend your answer and be able to explain "why" you chose these two options for Patti-Ann. (Note: Remember, this is about *positioning the company* for future success, not driving immediate revenues just yet.)

QUESTION 2: *From a sales and business development perspective,* please suggest two ways that Patti-Ann can effectively position Rockaway Construction for K–12 school construction projects in the first eighteen months of her arrival in Phoenix. (Something to consider: School construction projects are usually set out for public bidding.)

CHAPTER 9
Closing the Deal

You've got to be very careful if you don't know where you are going, because you might not get there.

— *Yogi Berra*

©djile/Shutterstock.com

CHAPTER OBJECTIVES

✓ Understand the difference between earning a commitment and closing a deal

✓ Discuss how closing the deal signifies a new stage of the sales life cycle

✓ Discover how a positive attitude and confidence can be the difference between good and great

✓ Learn effective questions designed to close the deal

✓ Explore why lowering your price to earn a customer may actually backfire

✓ Sharpen your negotiation skills and potentially make better deals in business

Robert is a seasoned sales professional with StageFire Network Systems (SNS). For the past two years he has been working closely with one of his top clients, CHI, a national call center company that specializes in banks with assets of $5 billion or more. During these two years Robert developed a close relationship with Jon Enwiller, Senior Vice President of I.T. at CHI. In fact, earlier in the year Robert and Jon completed a $350,000 deal to upgrade the network for CHI's regional facility in Toledo, Ohio.

After two long years and dozens of meetings, a series of edited proposals, and negotiations, the time had come for Jon and CHI to make a decision on their Tempe, Arizona, regional facilities. The time had also come for Robert to close the Tempe deal because his superiors were eager to see the fruits of his labors for the past two years.

There was a lot hanging in the balance on the closing of this particular Tempe deal–because, if all continued to go well–CHI was planning *an additional* two more network upgrades for their facilities in Florida and Oregon. Each network upgrade was not only $350,000 in new revenues for SNS, but also a $30,000 commission check for Robert–**paid upon each closing**.

The final proposal review for the Tempe project went well, and this was immediately followed by small talk between Jon and Robert around an initial deployment date. On the surface, Jon and Robert seemed to have a fairly straightforward deal: sign the contract and select a deployment date for the network upgrade. Jon said, "I have the authority to sign off on this contract, but how quickly can you get your team to get in here and begin upgrading the system?" Robert replied, "This would take approximately six to eight weeks, but only after receiving a signed

©Monkey Business Images/Shutterstock.com

contract." With May 1 just next week, the timing seemed ideal because Jon's goal was to have the network upgraded by July 1. This deadline was critical to CHI because several of their banking clients needed the software update in order to roll out new banking products for Q3 and Q4. If the July 1 deadline could not be met, CHI was considering holding off until January 1.

Jon thanked Robert and said that he would have the signed contract back to him in about one week. However, a few days later Robert received a call from Jon explaining that he was in the process of signing the contract but may have to pause for a few days because they just hired Lee Granquist, CHI's new Administrator for Sourcing and Contracts (ASC). This new ASC would play a key role in the Tempe network upgrade, as well as the future upgrades in Florida and Oregon. Therefore, Jon wanted to know if Robert had some time in the coming days to meet with Lee, allow him some time to review the Tempe proposal, ask questions about the network upgrade, and get up to speed with the process. Robert did not have a problem with meeting Lee, but he was slightly concerned that delays in a signed contract would negatively impact the July 1 deployment goal.

While the initial meeting with Lee and Robert went well, Lee had a fair amount of questions and concerns about the network upgrade. Lee asked Robert if he would be comfortable coming into the next Administrator team meeting at CHI to address a few concerns that Lee and his team had regarding the Tempe network roll-out. Robert quickly obliged, and promised he would attend the next meeting. The meeting was set for May 10. Later on that night Robert called Jon and briefed him on the meeting with Lee. Jon apologized for the contract delay, but reiterated that he could not sign the official contract until Lee and his team were comfortable.

On May 12 the meeting went fairly smooth, and Robert was able to answer most questions and alleviate the ASC team's major concerns. However, the one take-away was that Robert would agree to some basic contract changes, particularly the language about deliverables and quality control process. Robert said he would get back with his team at SNS and make those contract changes in approximately three to five business days. Although Robert knew he could get his team to quickly agree to the contract changes, he was concerned that another week would be lost in the process, resulting in a real time crunch for a July 1 deployment. Furthermore, Robert's operations team informed him that they have other clients to service during this time frame, and there was no longer a guarantee that a July 1 deadline could be honored.

CLOSING THE DEAL

In professional selling, "closing the deal" can be challenging and stressful. It should be noted that anyone seeking a career in professional sales should not expect the sales life cycle (and the commission checks) to be easy or fast, especially when the contracts are large. Obtaining a signed contract can be a long, difficult, and arduous task resulting in a sales professional experiencing a series of ups, downs, and setbacks. Some of the obstacles a professional sales representative may experience are budget timing, multiple decision-makers and signatures needed on a single contract, legal challenges requiring attorney involvement, financial approval from a CFO, internal politics, length of time for a company's formal purchasing "process," and of course the sales professional's ability to coordinate with his/her own operational teams (if they cannot deliver the product/service, meet customer deadlines, deliver quality, the sales professional will fail). In fact, Gartner research reports that firms with 100–500 employees have approximately seven decision-makers involved in the buying process (Tousley 2017).

In the chapter's opening story, what seemed to be a simple signature and deliverable date turned into a possible six-month delay. Many times these obstacles can be anticipated and planned for, but sometimes unforeseen circumstances can arise that can derail the sales process. Robert navigated the two-year sales process nicely, but the unforeseen variable of dealing with Lee had the potential to significantly delay or cancel the contract. Robert now had to work his sales magic with CHI and his own internal team to make sure a tight July 1 deadline can be honored. The story of Robert and CHI has many moving parts, and serves as a perfect introduction into Chapter 9 and *Closing the Deal*.

SIX WAYS TO IMPROVE YOUR ABILITY TO CLOSE THE DEAL

Let's discuss six ways to improve your ability to close the deal. But first, the authors of this textbook wanted to make a clear distinction between "obtaining a commitment" and "closing the deal." The terms are sometimes used interchangeably, but in reality serve two different outcomes. The term "obtaining a commitment" is commonly referred to in industries such as telemarketing, insurance, financial management, and national collegiate sales competitions for undergraduate students.

1. Obtaining a commitment.

Obtaining a commitment signifies the act of advancing the current sales dialogue to the next appropriate stage of the sales life cycle. Essentially, it means the buyer has agreed to a future meeting with the sales professional for the purposes of advancing the discussion.

> ### Obtaining a Commitment
> ───────────
> the act of advancing the current sales dialogue to the next appropriate stage of the sales life cycle.

Let's take a look at the insurance industry as an example. Insurance agents have two kinds of goals in their sales efforts: (1) obtaining quotes from their prospects, and (2) obtaining a signed insurance policy—turning a prospect into a client! An insurance agent may market to a commercial client in June of any given year, but the client may not be comfortable switching their insurance in the middle of the year. The prospect may prefer waiting until their renewal date in January. Therefore, the insurance agent and the prospect may agree to revisit the conversation in late December or early January, and the two parties can discuss a quote at that time. In this case, obtaining permission to get a quote in December or January is a small win for the agent because the customer <u>has agreed to meet again </u>to discuss a quote. Waiting for a renewal date is fairly common in the insurance industry, and therefore insurance *managers* like to see their representatives with a calendar full of follow-up commitments (or future meetings) for insurance quotes. While the insurance representative did not necessarily close the deal, per se, they did advance the conversation with the prospect and earned a commitment from the customer: permission to get a quote in the near future.

Many undergraduate universities compete in national collegiate sales competitions. One of the categories on the scoring matrix used by the judges is "obtaining a close or commitment." Since each competitor has approximately twenty minutes to perform in a sales role-play, they do not always have sufficient time to earn a signed contract—or formally close the deal. Therefore, if the student/competitor is successful in turning a sales pitch into a future meeting with the decision-maker, this often qualifies as (and is often referred to as) "a close." The student will receive favorable points for obtaining a commitment from the buyer in the role-play. However, if the buyer in the role-play refuses to meet again, or make another appointment, the judges may score the student poorly for their inability to earn a commitment—or a close. (In collegiate sales competitions the terms are often used interchangeably, but in the business world there is a difference between gaining a commitment and closing a deal.)

Closing the Deal

the act of obtaining a signed contract that signifies the end of a sales process and the beginning of a client management process.

Closing the deal is the act of obtaining a signed contract that signifies the end of a sales process and the beginning of a client management process. Using the insurance example above, if the agent follows up with the prospect in late December as promised, and provides a quote that potentially saves the prospect money (or adds more value to the policy), there is a reasonable chance the prospect will sign the new insurance policy and the agent will receive commission compensation for the closed deal. Once the deal is closed the sales process does not end for the insurance agent. The agent will always be looking for new products or services to sell to his current client base (i.e., additional services, life insurance, umbrella policies). Closing the deal signifies that the prospect has now become a paying customer, and the insurance agent shifts his/her approach from purely selling and pitching to

©Gustavo Frazao/Shutterstock.com

managing, growing, and protecting the client relationship (known as client retention). **Client retention** is all of the various activities that a professional sales representative–or his/her company—undertakes in an effort to retain the client's business.

✓ Retaining current clients is six to seven times less expensive than obtaining new ones (Kingwell 2015).

✓ It is 50 percent easier to sell to current customers versus new customers. (Farris, Bendle, Pfeifer, and Reibstein 2010)

✓ 80 percent of your company's future revenue will come from just 20 percent of your existing customers. (Tousley 2017)

Therefore, the authors highly recommend approaching prospects and clients twofold: the main goal is to obtain a signed contract (closing the deal) and earn their business; however, if the buyer is not ready to sign a contract (for whatever reason) the default goal should be to earn a commitment for that next conversation/meeting—even if it takes a couple of months to revisit the conversation. Never give up!

2. *Attitude and confidence.*

Having a positive *attitude and confidence* can significantly improve one's ability to close the deal. Dale Carnegie research studied the makings of top performers and what drives success. The research indicated three (3) main categories make up highly successful people: Knowledge, Skills, and Attitude. Knowledge accounted for approximately 10 percent of a person's success. The remaining 90 percent was Skills and Attitude. The perspective here is that many professionals place MOST of their time and energy into the category of Knowledge: we all take classes, watch seminars, attend conferences, read books, take lessons, and so on. Most professionals seek knowledge. Yet, 90 percent of what takes someone from good to great, or great to extraordinary is utilizing the skills we learned and developing a great attitude. Think about it: how many of us have not only taken the lesson, but went to the practice range and worked on the skills we learned? How many of us learned a few neat professional sales and sales management tricks right here in this textbook/class and are now practicing those behaviors in our personal and professional lives? And here is a powerful question for each of you: how many of you are actively and knowingly working to improve your attitude in life? The opportunity to differentiate—or ONE of the opportunities to differentiate—is to practice what we learn, and develop a great attitude that will carry us through difficult times. Many would make the argument that hiring someone with a great attitude is a much safer bet than hiring someone with a lot of knowledge and a bad

Client Retention

all of the various activities that a professional sales representative—or his/her company—undertakes in an effort to retain the client's business.

CHAPTER 9   Closing the Deal

attitude. It's no coincidence that a CEO, politician, or successful realtor each has an extraordinary ability to make customers feel that they are the most important person in the room. They make eye contact, they smile, and they are personable. Outwardly they seem polished and confident. You can be assured inwardly they have stress like everybody else: each of them probably has dozens of e-mails, voicemails, text messages, and urgent meetings piled up. Nonetheless, they condition themselves to have a great attitude when dealing with people right in front of them.

In preparation for this textbook, the authors interviewed Mr. Lou D'Amico, Business Manager at Cathedral Preparatory Seminary in Queens, New York. Cathedral has been consistently rated one of the top 50 Catholic High Schools in the United States. Students at Cathedral are required to wear business and formal attire to school. When asked how the dress code may or may not impact students' academic performance, D'Amico quickly responded, "I can tell you categorically that professional attire provides students a sense of self worth and confidence in their exchanges with faculty. Professional attire also impacts the perception the teachers have of the students—viewing them as young men and not boys. So the conversations tend to be elevated. At the same time, when we do have a jeans day or dress-down day, that is when we experience the most trouble in school. Students are less likely to get in trouble when they wear a suit, but put them in jeans and magically they become boys on a playground. Very true statement, and one of the reasons why we require professional attire." Additionally, in her book *Mind What You Wear*, Professor Karen Pine offers research that what you wear to work not only impacts the perception that others have on you, but also the perception you have of yourself. Professor Pine goes on to say that clothing "can change their mood and their thoughts" (Pine 2014). Take the State of the Union Address, for example. It is not uncommon for the President of the United States to wear a red tie in his address to the nation. Research indicates that red symbolizes power and projects confidence. Therefore, one way to improve attitude is to carefully consider what you wear to work.

Here are three ways to work on attitude and confidence:

A. Dress the part. If you want to be an FBI Agent, dress like an FBI Agent.

B. Begin every conversation—regardless of who you talk to—with "How are you?" Follow this up with a bright smile, and you will see the impact on people almost immediately!

C. Find the silver lining in everything negative. "I have to go to work tonight, but . . . I am also grateful that I have a job. Things could be worse."

Student Note

These behaviors may sound overly simplistic, but as you practice these more and more, you will begin to notice that people are drawn to confidence and positive attitudes. People want to be associated with winners.

CLASS EXERCISE

A savvy Sales Manager will assume the sales professional already has the requisite industry knowledge and/or education supporting why the company hired him/her in the first place. And it is well-documented that positive attitudes are often found in the most successful of people in our society. Using an industry that students can relate to (i.e., restaurant, retail, etc.) let's take 5–10 minutes and create a brief classroom discussion on how sales managers can: (a) identify several areas of someone's job that may cause an employee to carry a poor attitude, and then (b) using that same person/job identify what steps a manager can take to help improve the attitude of his/her employees in that respective role. For example, sometimes a bad tip—or no tip at all—can be the main factor for a waiter having a bad attitude that day/shift. Perhaps a savvy manager understands the value of a positive attitude in a restaurant and therefore gives a pep talk before every shift on keeping a positive attitude when a customer fails to leave a tip (many more customers will be coming into the restaurant that day. Do not let your whole shift become negatively impacted over one bad customer experience).

DID YOU KNOW

✓ The early bird gets the worm. 50 percent of sales go to the first salesperson to contact the prospect. (Tousley 2017)

✓ 84 percent of B2B decision-makers begin the buying journey with a referral. (Coleman 2016)

✓ 74 percent of buyers chose the company that was the first to add value. (Cernel 2016)

3. Ask for the Sale.

One of the most common mistakes sales professionals make is . . . simply *not asking* for the business, or the sale! Some research indicates that nearly 50 percent of all sales calls end without the sales professional asking for a sale (Lappe 2014). The true professional will listen to the client, identify the needs, offer solutions, and then ask for the business. Paycom's co-founder and Chief Sales Officer, Jeff York, says, "We train our sales force to state our objective very early in the sales meeting: that our goal here today is to earn your business and obtain a signed contract." Here are three ways a sales professional can ask for the business—every time:

A. "If we can solve your problems and provide solutions for less money, is there a reason you wouldn't move forward with us?"

B. "Based on everything I have heard from you today, here are three recommendations I have. Which one feels the best fit for you?"

C. "You had mentioned earlier that the current process is inefficient and negatively impacting productivity. What do you say we take this opportunity to improve the process and provide employees with the best tools?"

ETHICAL

Jesse was in a great mood. It was Labor Day Weekend and Jet Skis were going on sale at St. Peter's Outdoor Sports. Jesse had been eyeing a new Jet Ski all summer, but could not bring himself to pay top dollar for the machine. He knew that if he was patient, he would save anywhere between 20–40 percent off the retail price. Labor Day Weekend signified the end of the summer season, and arguably the best time to purchase a Jet Ski.

Upon arriving in the store, Jesse was introduced to Molly, St. Peter's top sales associate for six straight months. In fact, if she made top sales associate for a seventh straight month she stood to receive a bonus trip for two to the Bahamas. With Jesse and Molly clearly motivated to sign a deal on a Jet Ski, the stars seemed aligned that both would go home very happy people. It was Sunday, and already 5:00 p.m. The store was set to close at 6 p.m., and Molly had requested vacation for Monday as her family and friends were in town, and they had a nice day planned out on the lake.

After discussing several Jet Skis, Jesse seemed to really like the RM 650. Even better, the machine was on sale for 30 percent off—all weekend. "Okay Molly, I think I like the 650. But here's my process: $5,000 is a lot of money to spend. And I need to sleep on this. I'll be in when the store opens tomorrow, and we'll see if we can make a deal. Do you think the store will go any lower on the 650?" Molly smiled and agreed that the 650 was probably the best deal in the store. She also reiterated that the $5,000 was the rock-bottom price and non-negotiable. "Okay then, I will see you tomorrow morning, Molly. And we will take it from there."

Molly did not want to lose the sale to another sales associate. This sale alone virtually guaranteed her a fantastic start to a seventh consecutive month. But there was one problem, Jesse wanted to sleep on it, he was starting to walk out to his car, and she was not working the next day. "Jesse, wait. How certain are you that you want to purchase the 650?" Jesse turned around, took a deep breath and said, "Pretty damned sure. I've been eyeing this machine for four months now, and 30 percent is the best discount I will ever see. But, I am not spending $5,000 without sleeping on it. Why,

©stoatphoto/Shutterstock.com

what's up Molly?" With the store closing in twenty-five minutes, Molly could sense Jesse was not going to budge on a decision. Knowing her commission check would likely exceed $1,000, a thought came to her mind: "What if I offer him $300 cash back under the table? I bet that would make him purchase tonight. I could slip him $300 out of my own pocket, and still make $700 commission. Plus, this sale would help me remain on track for another successful month." The only problem was that the store policy clearly indicated that employees cannot leverage their commission checks to help a customer make a decision. For example, if Jesse began telling other people he got an additional $300 off the sale, then other customers may demand the same pricing and fairness.

What should Molly do?

A. Honor the store policy and honor Jesse's wishes to sleep on it. Tell Jesse she will not be here tomorrow and wish him luck. Effectively lose the deal.

B. Offer Jesse the $300 incentive, but kindly ask him to keep it quiet. Everybody wins.

C. Tell Jesse that she has put all the work in and really wants to see this transaction through. Put on her salesman cap and close the deal in the remaining 25 minutes.

D. Are there any other options you would recommend for Molly?

4. Create the fork in the road.

Creating a symbolic fork in the road is one way to make a clear distinction for the customer. This approach to selling and closing a deal requires that you highlight the negative impacts that the current service/product has on the customer, while simultaneously highlighting another path (forward) that is more efficient, cost effective, and has the client's short- and long-term interests at heart. Closing the deal under this process requires effective questions that leaves the buyer in an either/or proposition. For example:

A. "Bob, you had mentioned that this issue is costing your business $700 per month. That's $8,400 per year. Can you afford to lose $8,400 per year?"

B. "You said earlier that this manual process of managing time cards is costing you about 5 hours per week. That equates to 20 hours a month and 240 hours a year. If you had that time back, can you tell me what improvements you would make to the business?"

5. If you bring them on price alone, they will leave you on price alone.

When it is time to close the deal, one objection that likely arises is the price objection. When you are building a book of business, or a book of "good clients," we recommend avoiding lowering your fees to make a deal. There is a story of a nationally acclaimed realtor and a respected businessman (the latter who later went on to teach marketing and sales at a notable university). The businessman was ready to sell his house, but he wanted to hire his good friend and "pitbull" realtor, Mr. Robert. Here is how their conversation went:

BUSINESSMAN: "Robert, I want you to sell my house."

ROBERT: "Sure thing, I will come by, take pictures, and have it listed by tomorrow night. This house is in a gorgeous neighborhood with good schools. It will sell quickly, no problem."

BUSINESSMAN: "I know, all realtors say that, and I appreciate the optimism. But I have a question for ya: what will this cost me in realtor fees?"

ROBERT: "7%."

BUSINESSMAN: "Robert, on a $300,000 house, that is $21,000. That's a lot of money. I know some realtors who will do this for 5%. Can you go 5%?"

ROBERT: "No, and you do not want realtors who are willing to drop their fees."

BUSINESSMAN: "Why would that be a bad thing, Robert? They still stand to make $15,000. Isn't that still a win-win for everybody?"

ROBERT: "I charge 7%. And with that 7% you have a realtor who will demand every penny of the $300,000 that your house is worth. If a buyer comes in at $285,000, I am going to fight tooth and nail to get you the $300,000 listing price—which is $15,000 more that stays in your pocket. Now, if you hire another realtor who is willing to drop their own commissions from 7% to 5%, what do you think they will do as they represent YOUR money? A buyer will come in and offer $285,000, the realtor will urge you to take that deal or counter to $292,500. The buyer will counter to $290,000. You will both probably settle somewhere around $291,500–$292,000. Now at a 5% commission on $291,500, you will pay the realtor $14,575, and you will also have lost $8,000–$9,000 off the original sale price. That scenario—with a reduced commission—will cost YOU approximately $23,000–$25,000. If I list your house at $300,000, and demand that we get $300,000, it is true that you will pay me approximately $21,000 in commission, but you will NOT lose any money off of your listing. Under MY scenario, you earn an extra $2,000–$4,000. Could you use an extra $2,000–$4,000 in your pocket?"

BUSINESSMAN: "You make an excellent point. If I hire someone who is willing to reduce their own commission fees, why would they defend my money so aggressively when they won't defend their own?"

ROBERT: "Exactly my point! Now, what do you say you let me get to work and get this house sold for $300,000? It's worth every penny."

There are times in business or negotiations where it is appropriate to lower fees in order to close the deal. Charging a fair price and articulating the value of that price—like Robert did in the previous scenario—is the recommended business practice. Otherwise, if you build your business on lowest price alone, you stand to lose those same customers when a competitor offers a lower price than you.

NEGOTIATIONS

In the story above with Robert and the businessman selling his house we learned a valuable lesson that we can sometimes send the wrong message by easily dropping our fees. We also can see the value of standing strong and articulating to customers WHY your paying full fees equates to having the best in town representing you. But there are times that a sales professional and a client will negotiate.

For the purposes of this course, **The Art of Negotiations** is to never give something up without requesting/receiving something in return. Smart buyers, aggressive buyers, will sometimes low-ball you in negotiations. They do this for a variety of reasons: (1) they are confident and in no rush, so their style is to find a great deal; (2) they want to test the seller and see how desperate he/she is to sell; (3) some buyers simply feel better if they can get the price down. That simple.

To make our point let's assume you and your spouse are hosting a yard sale. One of the items you are trying to get rid of (or sell) is an ABC bike that is actually very popular. You bought the bike for $250 approximately 8 months ago, and have only used it one time. So you would like to get $200 for the bike since it is basically brand new. A buyer comes by and salivates that the bike he has wanted for a year is on sale for $200 and in mint condition. But, this is a yard sale so why not negotiate? Please read the scenario below, and keep in mind that buyers will not only throw a price at you, but then systematically try to meet you in the middle of whatever price is offered. For example:

> **BUYER:** "Hey, nice bike. I love those bikes. So you are asking $200?"

> **SELLER:** "Ya I got it for $250 but only used it once. It's like brand new. I figure $200 is fair."

> **BUYER:** "Hmmm. Would you go $100 in cash?"

Note: Now here starts the art of negotiations. The buyer is either testing you to see how desperately you are willing to get rid of this bike, or to see if there is any wiggle room for negotiations. Here is where the sellers often make mistakes and begin to show their hand.

Scenario 1 (weak negotiator):

> **SELLER:** "$100? I don't think I can go $100. It's a brand new bike. How about $150?"

> **BUYER:** "$150? I don't know. For another $100 I get get a brand new one that has never been used, and probably even have a factory warranty for a year. No. The most I will go is $120."

> **SELLER:** "The bike is practically brand new and you should not have any issues for a while. How about we meet in the middle and go $135?"

Note: Notice how the buyer was able to continuously lure the seller downward, and now in a position to settle on $135 for a $250 bike? But yet, the seller never made efforts to see how badly the buyer WANTED the bike. Now let's consider scenario 2 and a real pro!

Scenario 2 (strong negotiator)

SELLER: "$100? I don't think I can go $100. It's a brand new bike. The price is already knocked $50 off. So no, I am going to stick with the $200 price. It will sell."

Note: the seller is in a strong position. Here's why: either the buyer will begin to show he/she really, really wants this bike and come WAY up close to the $200 mark—or—the buyer will walk away. If the buyer decides to walk away, the seller can suggest: "Make me a better offer than $100" and get the negotiations back on track.

BUYER: "I love this bike but I do not want to pay $200. Would you go $150?"

SELLER: "How about this. My spouse is not going to let me go $150 on a bike we just bought for $250. Now I can see you want this bike. I can go down another $10, but I need you to work with me here. How about we go $190, which is now $60 off the sale price, and you buy this helmet I purchased with the bike (and never used) for an additional $15. For $205 you get a brand new bike and helmet that has not left the box."

BUYER: "I do like the bike, but not feeling quite comfortable at $190. Would you go $180 if I take the helmet too?"

SELLER: "My spouse is going to freak out if we don't get most of our asking price for this bike. I'll tell you what: I will go $185 final price, but I need you to purchase the helmet, and manual air pump that attaches to the rim of the bike. I never used it, and when you are out on the road you will see how valuable it is to have a pump if your air pressure gets low. All 3 for $205."

In scenario 2 we are learning the valuable lesson of never giving up the price for a product or service without getting something in return. Imagine you are a software sales representative selling to a CFO. The CFO has no issues with the $30,000 per year cost of leasing the software, but has a difficult time agreeing to pay your $20,000 installation fee. The CFO may ask you to accept $10,000. A weak negotiator would request that the CFO meet at $15,000. And a savvy CFO would come back with $12,500 (with the mind-set that you both met in the middle each time during the process). A smart negotiator—or one who took this course—would say to the CFO: "I could MAYBE talk to my boss about considering $19,000. But I am going to need a 2-year lease commitment instead of 1-year." The point we are making here is: keep your prices high and strong, and if you DO come down in price, or have to negotiate, try to get the buyer to throw in additional incentives. You will notice that this method works in BOTH your personal lives and professional lives.

6. *Identify concerns BEFORE you part ways.*

Imagine this scenario: You send in your resume and are soon called for a job screening by an HR representative. The first interview goes well, and a few days later you receive a favorable notice that the local department supervisor would like to have a round 2 interview with you. The second interview goes reasonably well, and one week later you receive a call that the department manager would like to have one final interview with you. During the final interview you seem to articulate the answers to all of the tough questions that the department manager has for you. The meeting comes to an end, and the manager thanks you for the visit and politely asks if you have any final questions for her before the two of you part ways.

In this scenario the most common mistake candidates make is that they fail to identify—or uncover—any lingering concerns that the hiring manager may have in mind. The concern could be your GPA is slightly lower than the company's "desired" minimum. The concern could be that you had two jobs in the last three years, and this is not quite sitting well with the manager. Here's the point: you are in round 3 of a job interview process. All of the cards are on the table. You are looking to get this job (or close this deal).

The window to address ANY concerns is right here, right now! Therefore, the authors recommend uncovering and addressing any potential concerns that the buyer has . . . before you part ways.

To see how to effectively uncover concerns, let's continue the scenario from above. The manager thanks you and asks if you have any final questions for her. Instead of saying no thank you, shaking hands, and exiting, you decide to ask one final question: "I do have one final question if you are comfortable answering: are there any concerns—or remaining questions that you would like further clarity on—that would prevent us from moving forward in this process?" Think about it: if the hiring manager says, "No, I do not have any concerns at this time," technically there should be no reason that they not hire you (you went through the entire process, the boss said they had no concerns—it's reasonable to assume you are in a great position to get the job!). However, what if the hiring manager said to you: "Well, you are an incredibly talented young man. But our minimal desired GPA is a 3.4. Your GPA is a 3.2, and this does put me at odds with others we have hired in the past." Think about it: you have about 15 seconds to relieve this concern—or—the two of you will part ways and possibly never speak again. In that 15 seconds, what if you said: "Ok, thank you for sharing that concern. Would you take into consideration that my freshman year was the first time I ever moved away from home, and that I did not do well academically that first semester? I was 18, and while I passed all of my classes, my GPA was a 2.5. However, my Sophomore, Junior, and Senior years of college were a 3.6, 3.9, and 4.0 respectively. And my core courses were a 3.9. Would you take into consideration that my last 3 years demonstrate that my commitment to academics and achievement have far exceeded the 3.4 minimal requirement?"

Wow! What a close. While this does not guarantee receiving the job offer it DOES give the hiring manager some ammunition to overlook the 3.4 GPA minimum requirement. She is in a position to defend her decision because you took the time to uncover the issue. Now think about professional selling. You have a client who meets with you two to three times and says, "I'll be in touch." Allowing them to go through their decision process is acceptable and appropriate. But there is something powerful in knowing that whatever concerns they may have . . . that you understand what they are before you part ways. Their concern could be financing. Their concern could be making that first payment in February (because March is when he receives his bonus every year). Your odds of closing the deal will improve by uncovering the concern.

CHAPTER SUMMARY

There is a clear distinction between obtaining a commitment and closing the deal. Obtaining a commitment is a form of closing the deal in that it ensures that the sales dialogue moves to the next stage of the sales process. However, closing the deal signifies that a product or a service has been exchanged for money, and that the prospect has now moved along the sales life cycle to the client retention phase. It is cheaper to retain an existing client than to market to a prospect, and it is 50 percent "easier" to sell new products or services to an existing client than a prospect.

A professional sales representative's attitude and confidence is a major factor in his/her ability to close deals. Research shows that most professionals work hard at obtaining new knowledge and improving their skills, but the elite tend to spend time working on their attitude and confidence. There are a variety of ways to begin practicing these behaviors such as how you dress and taking the time to build rapport/pleasantries.

A huge mistake many sales professionals make is simply not asking for the business. Research shows that almost 50 percent of sales professionals fail to ask for a signed contract. Yet, we have the opportunity to ask for the business 100 percent of the time. Creating a fork in the road is a method that allows the prospect to see two symbolic paths: one of continued pain and

©Backgroundy/Shutterstock.com

waste, and another of efficiency and prosperity. It begs the question: Which path would you like to take? Lowering your price to earn business is not the recommended strategy for closing deals. If customers only come to you on low price, you can expect they will leave you when a competitor offers a lower price. Therefore, define your worth and articulate why the prospect/customer is better off doing business with you versus the competition. In the case of Robert and the businessman, the businessman stood to make MORE money by paying higher commissions. Funny how that works.

The Art of Negotiations is to have the mind-set to only give up something with an expectation to receive something else in return. If the hiring salary was $45,000–$55,000 there is nothing wrong or unprofessional with respectfully telling a hiring manager, "$45,000 is a bit lower than I was expecting. Can we shoot for $52,000 with at least 2 additional days of vacation?" You will not always get what you want, but in a lifelong journey of negotiations (and you will have many!) you will be far more effective utilizing negotiation skills such as the ones we discussed here in this textbook.

Lastly, closing the deal is a mind-set, and the best professionals are the ones who always seek to obtain a signed contract, but know how to keep the sales conversations alive when a customer says "not now," or "I will get back in touch with you." It's acceptable to ask the client (or prospective employer) if there are any concerns holding him/her back from moving forward—before parting ways.

REFERENCES

Cernel, Shelley, 2016. "4 Keys to Conversations that Advance the Sale." Salesforce blog. January 28. https://www.salesforce.com/blog/2016/01/conversations-advance-the-sale.html

Coleman, Steve. 2016. "Referrals top when it comes to B2B purchasing decisions." Perivan Technology. https://www.perivantechnology.co.uk/sales-blog/referrals-top-when-it-comes-to-b2b-purchasing-decisions

Farris, Paul, Bendle, Neil, Pfeifer, Phillip, and Reibstein, David. 2010. *Marketing Metrics*. Upper Saddle River, NJ: Pearson Education, Inc.

Kingwill, Ian. 2015. Linkedin. "What is the cost of customer acquisition vs customer retention?" https://www.linkedin.com/pulse/what-cost-customer-acquisition-vs-retention-ian-kingwill

Lappe, Neal. 2014. "How to Know When to Ask for the Sale." Webstrategies. https://www.webstrategiesinc.com/blog/knowing-ask-sale

Pine, Karen J. 2014. *Mind What You Wear: The Psychology of Fashion*. Amazon Kindle.

Tousley, Scott J. 2017. "107 Mind-Blowing Sales Statistics That Will Help You Sell Smarter." Gartner Group. https://blog.hubspot.com/sales/sales-statistics

9

HOMEWORK

On an idle Tuesday in March, Caroline could not help swinging into the local Starbucks to grab a quick cup of coffee to go. As she was standing in line a gentleman quietly whispered to her, "Whatever happened to the days of just ordering a regular cup of coffee, huh?" The two exchanged smiles and Caroline said, "I know! All these creative names and options. If you said 'regular coffee' they may look at you like you have two heads."

As Caroline looked away she could not help but to recognize this gentleman from somewhere. After approximately forty-five seconds of trying to recall where she had met him before, she simply could not place the name with the face. "Have we met before?" Caroline said with a big smile. "Uh, maybe" the gentleman said. "It's quite possible. I do work for a fairly visible person."

"Okay, and who is this 'person' you work for?" Caroline responded.

The gentleman extended his hand and said, "Hi, I'm Mark Pfeifle, and I work for the Governor. I travel with the Governor quite a bit so it is not uncommon for people to recognize my face."

After a few brief pleasantries Mark was surprised to hear that Caroline was a senior sales rep for "Pens Galore," a major pen company with revenues over $500 million a year. It just so happened that Mark was recently tasked with ordering pens for the Governor's Office. These pens would be used for the Governor signing legislation on television, and then the Governor would give the pens away as gifts to observers in the room. Mark requested that Caroline come by the Governor's office in two days to make her sales pitch. As Mark was leaving he mentioned that he has a limited budget, but he has permission to spend more than the average pen, of course. The pens should be of a quality that are commensurate with the Office of the Governor. The optics of the pens should also be taken into consideration because there will be news media taking pictures and recording video.

QUESTION 1: Is this enough information for Caroline? If not, what other questions would you recommend Caroline ask Mr. Pfeifle?

QUESTION 2: What advice do you have for Caroline to close the deal when she makes her sales pitch at the Governor's Office?

CHAPTER 10
Clients for Life

Profits were not our immediate goal, but the natural and appropriate outcome of doing everything else right.

— *Dick DeVos*

©fizkes/Shutterstock.com

CHAPTER OBJECTIVES

✓ Explore the concept of client retention as a mind-set in professional sales

✓ Discuss how retaining clients is cheaper than obtaining new ones

✓ Explore five new tactics and strategies for retaining customers

✓ Discuss the benefits of retaining clients

Steve and Wendy Hansen left the bank with smiles from ear to ear. They were just pre-approved to purchase a home. It was now time to go shopping with their realtor, Kathy Wilson. After two months of looking at houses they finally found the home of their dreams. Kathy suggested they go back to the bank to get their formal home loan papers updated because they were scheduled to move into their new home in just forty-five days.

Since two months had passed, the bank was required to re-check the credit scores and make sure nothing "new" popped up on their credit report. The banker also requested recent pay stubs and a recent bank statement. When the credit was reprocessed the banker's faced was flushed and his eyes popped wide open. "What's wrong?" Wendy asked. "Did one of you buy a new car recently, in the last thirty days or so?" the banker replied. Steve said "I did. Why? Is that a problem?" The banker explained that a new car means more debt, lower credit scores, and tighter financial ratios. This could potentially disqualify them from the loan. "You said we were pre-approved. You never said anything about stopping our lives and not taking out any new loans," Steve said angrily. The banker said he was sorry and should have explained this better, and that he would need to visit with the underwriter immediately to see if this loan could still be approved.

Twenty-four hours later Steve and Wendy received a call from the banker. "Good news! We can still approve you for this home loan. The ratios were tight, but we are still okay. However, I will need recent pay stubs to show that you're still employed, and I need a recent bank statement

©Alexander Supertramp/Shutterstock.com

to reflect that you still have a $10,000 down payment." Later on that day Steve and Wendy arrived at the bank, and upon handing over the pay stubs and bank statement, the banker once again appeared disturbed. "What? What's the problem now?" Wendy snapped. The banker held up the bank statement and said, "Your bank statement says there's only $7,000 in the bank right now. You're supposed to have at least $10,000 in the bank to be used for the down payment. If you don't have at least $10,000, then we may have another problem approving the loan." Steve calmly explained that it is a misunderstanding. He lent his brother $3,000 a few days ago, but he did not think much of it because his brother was scheduled to pay him back in a few weeks, plenty of time before the loan closing.

Once again, the banker said, "I pre-approved you on the condition that you had $10,000 in the bank. You no longer have that money in the bank. I cannot move the loan forward in the hopes that your brother will pay you back in a few weeks. Furthermore, when he DOES pay you back we need a signed letter from him that he is paying you back and not lending you money for the new house. If he is lending you money then we need to count it as another loan against you." Frustrated and embarrassed, Steve and Wendy stood up, announced they are going to another bank, and walked out.

CLIENT RETENTION

Up until now the textbook has covered many critical professional sales concepts such as building trust, networking, prospecting, selling, effective communication, closing the deal, and more. Each of these concepts are also stages of the sales life cycle with your customers. Each concept/stage of the sales life cycle takes time, effort, preparation, and persistence. It's not easy, and the top performers work hard to achieve success. Once a sales professional actually obtains the signed contract and turns a prospect into a client . . . it is time to make them customers for life! Research indicates that retaining current clients is six to seven times less expensive than obtaining new ones (Kingwill 2016).

In the story above—which commonly happens in mortgage banking—proper expectations between the banker and the Hansens were not set, and many of the concepts listed above were ignored. A true mortgage professional would have pre-approved the customers, and then wisely explained the importance of the Hansens to not intentionally change the credit or financial package that initially resulted in a pre-approval. Setting expectations with clients is a watershed concept that strikes at the very foundation of clients for life. The authors will spend more time on the concept of setting expectations later in the chapter.

FIVE WAYS TO RETAIN CUSTOMERS

1. Lifetime value of a customer.

Consider the **lifetime value of a customer**—not the single transaction. The employees at Starbucks work hard. From early in the morning and well into the evening they assist scores of people coming into the store to purchase their favorite coffee, latte, or drink of choice. In fact, it's not uncommon to find loyal customers who come into Starbucks four to five times a week, spending an average of $5 each time. (Some of you reading this textbook might even be thinking "Yep, that's me!") Let's consider what happens when a loyal customer has a bad experience at Starbucks and decides to never come back.

Lifetime Value of a Customer

the estimated revenues that a business will derive from the lifetime relationship with a customer.

Let's assume an honest mistake and the coffee/drink simply came out wrong, and now the employee and customer exchange a few harsh words. Frustrated, the customer storms off and decides to never come back to Starbucks again. Some employees may view this as a $4 loss and one less annoying customer. But now let's consider the **lifetime value** of what just transpired: If this frustrated customer spent an average of $20–$25 per week, and there are fifty-two weeks in the year, then Starbucks stands to lose approximately $1,000–$1,300 in revenue in one year. Over a twenty-year time period this equates to approximately $20,000–$26,000. Now, when you factor in cross-selling opportunities (coffee cups, gifts for friends, bringing new friends—new customers—into the store for coffee), that dollar amount conceivably rises to a staggering $50,000 or more over a twenty-year timeframe. A company like Starbucks cannot afford to have too many loyal customers walk out. Any business-savvy employee, manager, or corporate executive would agree that "making it right" with the customer would save the company tens of thousands of dollars in lost revenues—all because of one bad cup of coffee and one bad experience.

By understanding *and appreciating* the lifetime value of a customer, sales professionals will be far more inclined to "make it right" when those awkward customer service moments come along.

2. *Critics are our friends.*

Benjamin Franklin once said, "Critics are our friends, they show us our faults." By all accounts human nature is to avoid controversy, and most research would demonstrate that employees prefer to shy away from controversy with a customer because they do not want to get fired from their job. However, if only 4 percent of customers complain and 96 percent walk away quietly, the reality is businesses have a very small group of customers willing to provide raw feedback when there is a problem (Thomas Consulting 2017). It's difficult to "make it right" when the customers are not likely to come forward. So the customers who do come forward to complain may be a valuable listening channel for a business. Therefore, it is recommended that professional sales representatives embrace customer dissatisfaction and view it as an opportunity to retain their customers.

The customer service department at Dell calls new customers very early in the sales process asking how their experience is going thus far. The intent is to catch customer dissatisfaction early, make it right, and retain customers for life. Customers are left with a phone number and are told what to do and who to call if there are any future issues with the new computer. One way to retain customers is to embrace criticism as a means to constantly make improvements.

3. *Set expectations.*

The beauty of expectations is that they can be managed. As we discussed in the opening story of this chapter, setting expectations is a watershed concept in retaining or losing customers. For starters, setting expectations eliminates uncertainty and almost immediately improves trust between a client and a business. Additionally, if there are any pitfalls with a product or a service—such as hidden fees—discussing with the clients upfront is not just the right thing to do, it's smart business!

Here is the most effective way to set expectations with clients: first, put the expectations in writing using simple and clear language. Second, review the expectations with the client and allow them time to ask questions about the process and things to come. For example, if underwriting a car or home loan takes five to seven business days to render a decision, then express that in simple written terms, and then verbally explain that five to seven business days equates to at least one full week, and possibly two weeks depending on which day of the week the process begins. (If you are having this conversation on Thursday, June 1, underwriting may not render a decision until Monday, June 12. To a customer, this can seem like a long time, but if you put it in writing and verbally explain it the client is less likely to complain during the seven business days.)

4. *It's hard to fire someone you like.*

There's a story of an insurance agent named Dave who had his series 6 and 7 licenses, and was also licensed to sell life insurance. He made a list of his top twenty-five clients, and made sure that each of those twenty-five clients received three personal touches per calendar year. If one of them had a baby, Dave was one of the first to the hospital with flowers. If there was a birthday party for any of the children, he made sure to drop by with a small gift. If the circus was in town, Dave would e-mail his top twenty-five and remind them that he had free tickets. And if he was driving by and saw his top clients outside, he made it a point to pull over and shake everyone's hand and give hugs when appropriate.

With such a personal and effective strategy, Dave made it next to impossible for his clients to fire him and leave for the competition. For all his faults, Dave was a good guy who knew how to personalize such an important service such as property insurance, life insurance, and retirement accounts. Put simply, Dave understood and appreciated *clients for life*. The authors recommend that as aspiring sales professionals you develop a likeability strategy, because it's hard to fire someone you like. And it's a brilliant way to keep customers for life!

5. *Customer loyalty program.*

This is a brilliant tactic that many businesses use these days, and a strategy that Starbucks has mastered. The Starbucks strategy is simple: we hang out where our customers hang out . . . their cell phones! With more than 1 million (and rising) customers subscribed to the Starbucks rewards app, customers are able to either transfer money into the app or transfer gift card dollars into the app. The convenience of scanning your cell phone to pay for coffee provides the *impression* that coffee is quick and free. The benefit

©BestStockFoto/Shutterstock.com

to Starbucks? You have more than 1 million customers returning over, and over, and over again.

Starwood's Preferred Guest Program is a loyalty program that focuses on perceived value versus real cost. In other words, late check-outs, free Internet, and room upgrades are all highly perceived values for their customers (who doesn't mind a room upgrade upon check-in? Or a late check-out the following morning?). Little monetary cost to the hotel, but a big win for the customer.

In professional sales, it may seem more difficult to offer clients a formal customer loyalty program. But keep in mind that a loyalty program is all about making customers feel appreciated and valued. According to a study by Rockefeller Corporation 68 percent of customers stop buying because of "perceived indifference." In other words, there is a sense the seller (or seller's company) does not care about the customer. It's fascinating to think so many of us work so hard to get a relationship in the door, but too often allow it to slip away due to a perception we do not care. Reward loyal customers! Here are two ways your local sales office or department can create its own customer loyalty program:

A. Purchase a block of tickets to the local minor league baseball team (or the like). Rotate your top twenty to forty clients, and randomly reach out and ask if they are interested in taking their families to a game. Depending on the city, the cost of a block of four tickets for twenty games will run approximately $1,200. Clients love a random phone call with free tickets.

B. Dentist or children's doctor's office: reward children actual points for checking in on time, cooperating, and allow them to either cash out the points for a small prize, or build up the points for a larger prizes like movie tickets or gift cards. Creating a positive experience for the children at the dentist or doctor's office unquestionably pleases the parents.

DID YOU KNOW

✓ Increasing customer retention rates by 5 percent increases profits 25 to 95 percent (Reichheld & Schefter 2000)

✓ Companies who listen to their customers see 40 percent better growth in customer retention than those who don't (Miller Heiman Group)

✓ 65 percent of a company's business comes from existing customers (Evans and Lindsay 2012)

✓ According to a study done by Rockefeller Corporation, the number one reason customers stop buying is "perceived indifference" (Rockefeller Corporation)

ETHICAL

Stephanie Dietrich walked into the local hardware store looking for an air pressure machine for her husband as a Father's Day gift. She needed to make this purchase quickly as she only had fifteen minutes before having to pick up her daughter at school. Upon seeing Stephanie pacing up and down the aisle, one of the sales associates—who was relatively new on the job—approached her and asked if she could use some assistance. Stephanie appreciated the gesture and said, "Hi! Thank you. I am looking for an air pressure machine for my husband as a Father's Day gift. I'm in a bit of a rush and need to pick up my daughter. We are on a tight budget, and the most I can spend is $75. I see you have some really nice air pressure machines for $100–$125, but we are going through a really rough time financially right now and I need to keep this to a $75 purchase maximum."

After five minutes of reviewing several possibilities with the sales associate, Stephanie decided to go with the Longboat 350 Air Compressor. Even better, it was priced at $69.99. Stephanie thanked the sales associate and made her way to the cashier. As the sales associate walked away, one of his colleagues gave him a high five and said, "Wow, it looks like you helped the customer! What did she buy?" The associate explained that it was an air pressure Longboat 350, and that the customer had a $75 tight budget and seemed to be fairly comfortable with the final decision. The colleague said, "Ah, the Longboat! We usually have a tough time selling those. Customers get frustrated because it's the only brand over there that requires you to purchase all of the ancillary pieces and air nozzle independently. And that costs another $52! Almost costs as much as the Longboat itself. She will spend way more than $75 to get that thing running."

Shocked at what he just heard, the sales associate noticed that Stephanie already paid the cashier and was putting the Longboat in a bag to carry out. The associate also recalled Stephanie saying that this is a Father's Day gift, and that their family was on a really tight budget due to some rough financial times. As she tied the bag, Stephanie looked at the associate and said, "Thank you so much. You've been really helpful. Gotta go get my kid, bye now!"

What should the sales associate do?

1. Race up to the front and disclose that the Longboat 350 will not work without another $52 in parts and pieces?

2. Let it go. Stephanie was in a rush, and she asked for help buying an air compressor under $75, and that's exactly what you did.

CLASS EXERCISE

1. What does it say about the character of the associate if he allows Stephanie to walk out of the store? About the character of the store and its employees?

2. What does it say about the character of the associate if he stopped Stephanie before leaving the store? Does it show incompetence? Or does it show that he/they are good people? Keep in mind the customer is in a rush to pick up her child.

3. What would you tell your employee to do?

CHAPTER SUMMARY

Some research indicates that retaining clients is six to seven times less expensive than obtaining new ones. Furthermore, the profit margin from repeat clients dramatically improves company bottom lines. Remember, even with a 90 percent client retention rate—which is excellent in many industries—your company is still bleeding 10 percent per year. The main reason customers stop buying is because they perceive indifference in the relationship that they have with you . . . or your company. Understanding and appreciating the lifetime value of a customer is one of the smartest training exercises a company can provide its new employees. As we mentioned in the Starbucks example, making a customer happy with a $4 cup of coffee can result in sales of $25,000–$50,000 in a twenty-year time span.

Research indicates that 96 percent of customers will never share their frustrations with employees. This means that businesses have about 4 percent of their customers willing to share raw issues and problems as they arise. As sales professionals, we should welcome the criticism of our clients. The sooner they share the information with us, the sooner we can improve the process and ultimately protect the relationship for life. Setting proper expectations with clients is arguably the foundation of earning customers for life. Setting expectations removes uncertainty and disarms frustration. Furthermore, setting expectations improves trust between the customer and the representative.

©Olivier Le Moal/Shutterstock.com

It's true: the more we like somebody, the harder it is to fire them. One way to earn customers for life is to improve the likeability factor with the client. There is a variety of ways to approach the likeability factor, and hopefully our story of "Dave" drove home how simple it can be to deploy such a strategy. A loyalty rewards program is a brilliant way to capture new clients, induce future buying behaviors with the clients, and retain their business for many years to come. While many of the larger companies such as Starbucks have advanced software and marketing strategies supporting their worldwide loyalty programs, the concept of customer loyalty is actually really simple and can be deployed by any small office with reasonable financial investment. The concept is to make clients feel special and to have a positive experience. If you can implement these tactics into your everyday customer management strategy, clients are far less likely to leave you and will be your "Clients for Life."

REFERENCES

Evans, J. R. and Lindsay, W. M. 2012. *Managing for Qualify and Performance Excellence*. Boston: Cengage Learning.

Kingwill, Ian. 2015. Linkedin. "What is the cost of customer acquisition vs customer retention?" https://www.linkedin.com/pulse/what-cost-customer-acquisition-vs-retention-ian-kingwill

Miller Heiman Group. http://blog.clientheartbeat.com/customer-retention/

Reichheld, Frederick and Schefter, Phil. 2000. "The Economics of E-Loyalty." Harvard Business School. http://hbswk.hbs.edu/archive/1590.html

Thomas Consulting. 2017. "Infinite Value of Customer Intelligence." http://www.thomasconsultingwins.com/category/client-retention/

10 HOMEWORK

In the fall of 2000, Minneapolis insurance agent, Dan Cole, was introduced to the Detrick family. Just starting out their married life together the Detricks quickly found themselves in need of home and car insurance. Since Mr. Cole was a referral from a friend, it was not a difficult choice to sign the paperwork with Dan Cole.

Two years later the Detricks had their first child. Sure enough, Dan Cole arrived at the hospital to meet the new Detrick. Now there was talk of adding a reasonable amount of life insurance and a college savings plan. Mr. Cole had licenses to provide both of those services, and the business relationship began to naturally deepen with time and relationship building. Several years later the Detricks had two more children and purchased a larger house to accommodate the spacing needs. Dan came to the hospital for both children, and even sent a housewarming gift for the new home. Once again the Detricks and Mr. Cole found themselves revisiting the topic of expanded life insurance policies and additional college savings plans for the children.

In 2013 the Detricks were transferred to Denver, Colorado, for work-related purposes. As they searched for homes in the Denver area, they realized that they would need home and auto insurance, but also roll over their 401K from the former company. Dan Cole was licensed in Denver, so he ensured the Detricks that he had all of their insurance and investment needs covered.

Ms. Detrick asked her husband a couple of fair questions: "How do we know Dan's insurance is competitive with the Denver insurance market? Shouldn't we at least get a couple quotes from local agents to make sure Dan Cole's Minneapolis rates are competitive? And will we ever see Dan Cole again? What if we have questions in the future about college savings plans? Or what if we have questions about our life insurance?" Since the Detricks had remained clients of Dan Cole since 2000, they decided to give it a shot and keep all of their insurance and financial investments with Dan Cole—for now.

QUESTION 1: If you were insurance agent Dan Cole do you think it is best to keep the Detricks as clients? Or would you recommend referring them to a local agent in Denver?

QUESTION 2: What specifically can insurance agent Dan Cole do all year to keep the Detricks as customers for life?

CHAPTER 11
What's Next . . . for the Sales Professional

If I had asked people what they wanted, they would have said faster horses.

— Henry Ford

©Andrey_Popov/Shutterstock.com

CHAPTER OBJECTIVES

- ✓ Explore how professional sales skills are similar to the skills of executives
- ✓ Discuss what it means to manage other sales professionals
- ✓ Explore the term "leadership" and what it means in business
- ✓ Discuss the difference between a leader and manager in business

As we enter the final chapter of this textbook and reflect on the key concepts and secrets to a successful career in sales, the authors felt compelled to draw a comparison from the impressive skills that make up a successful sales professional to the requisite skills of leaders and managers. According to *Forbes,* approximately 20 percent of Fortune 500 CEO's started out in sales and marketing roles (Savitz 2011).

Successful sales professionals make great leaders because they put into practice many of the same behaviors and skills necessary to lead a team, a department, or even a company. Professional sales representatives have walked the walk. For example, successful sales professionals understand the value of developing high levels of trust with other people. Managers and leaders in companies must establish a culture of trust with their employees. Another example is a leader's ability to think strategically. Successful sales professionals spend their entire careers developing strategic initiatives that work (and they have learned—many times very painfully—what strategies do NOT work). Steve Jobs famously said that leaders and entrepreneurs must "stay hungry." Well, just ask any successful sales professional about hunger, and you will likely hear: we eat what we kill. If we aren't hunting, we don't eat.

As we address the topic of "what's next" for your career in sales, let's take a closer look at what it means to be a sales manager—or in its simplest form what it means to be in "management." **Management** is the organization and coordination of the activities of a business—such as creating or executing corporate policy and organizing, planning, controlling, and directing an organization's resources in order to achieve defined goals. At the basic level, managers are hired to make sure employees are following through with their job description and/or "doing their job." While a title may signify that someone is in charge, it does not signify that they are providing leadership.

> ### *Management*
> the organization and coordination of the activities of a business—such as creating or executing corporate policy and organizing, planning, controlling, and directing an organization's resources in order to achieve defined goals.

Leadership is different from management because leadership encompasses the ability to inspire others. Therefore, to be a leader or to provide **leadership** is a process of social influence which maximizes the efforts *of others* towards achievement of a goal. Managed employees will perform five tasks (or the minimal required) at work because they are required to do it. Inspired employees will perform ten tasks because they are influenced to advance themselves, the team, the company, and its customers! The old adage is that inspired employees turn out the lights when they leave the room—they know it's saving their business and their company's money.

In John Maxwell's *The 5 Levels of Leadership* he talks about the difference in leadership at every level starting with Position, and moving up to Permission, Production, People Development, Pinnacle (Maxwell 2011). In level 1 you are a leader because of the position you have earned: supervisor, team lead, manager. Employees will follow that leader because of their position or title, and nothing more. These are the least effective leaders. At the Permission level the leader has demonstrated an elevated ability to develop relationships with employees resulting in staff who follow because they want to (not have to). In level 2 leaders have built stronger relationships because of their ability to listen, observe, and learn.

Level 3, 4, and 5 leaders are less common and see past the moment. Level 3 leaders understand the value of creating momentum with their employees. Maxwell says momentum and excitement in employees helps avoid 80 percent of the corporate problems. At the Production level employees tend to NOT get stuck when obstacles arise. Level 4 leaders develop those around them. For example: First, the leader does the job his/herself. If a leader is going to develop others he/she must be able to do what they teach. Second, the leader does the job but takes the follower with him/her. The follower observes, asks questions, and is basically mentored. In step 3 of people development the follower performs the duties, but this time the leader watches and observes. The leader may suggest a tweak or slight improvement, but for the most part the follower operates at their own capacity. In step 4 the follower performs the role alone, without assistance from the leader. They "just do it." Lastly, in step 5 of Maxwell's people development, the new leader is tasked with teaching the five steps to the next leader. They produce the next leader.

Level 5 of Maxwell's "5 Levels of Leadership" is called the Pinnacle. Only 1 percent of leaders ever reach this level of leadership. At the Pinnacle level employees follow the leader because they have the utmost respect for what the leader has accomplished on their long journey. These leaders have not just passed through the first 4 levels of leadership and have done exceptionally well in their careers, but have repeatedly achieved success time and time again. Level 5 is a lifetime journey, and these leaders are men and women we admire the most.

> ## *Leadership*
> a process of social influence which maximizes the efforts of others towards achievement of a goal.

The Five Levels of Leadership

5 **Pinnacle**
Most people never arrive at this level. This is attained through a lifetime of proven leadership. People follow you because of who you are and what you represent.

4 **People Development**
The leader empowers others. Successors are identified. Followers personally grow through mentorship of the leader. People follow you because of what you have done for them.

3 **Production**
Results matter here. People come together to accomplish a purpose. People follow you because of what you have done for the organization.

2 **Permission**
Leading with the heart and not the head. This requires meaningful relationships. People follow you because they want to.

1 **Position**
Basic entry level leadership. People follow you because they have to.

Tabs adapted from ©seamuss/Shutterstock.com and text ©Kendall Hunt Publishing Company

---

CLASS EXERCISE

1. Discuss what it was like to work for someone at level 1 in John Maxwell's 5 levels of leadership.

2. Have you ever worked for a leader who brought out the best in you? What was it that they said or did to make you feel inspired to do more in that role?

3. Discuss with your group what level you believe you are at in Maxwell's 5 levels.

FOUR WAYS YOU CAN WORK ON YOUR LEADERSHIP SKILLS AND RISE UP THROUGH MAXWELL'S 5 LEVELS OF LEADERSHIP

1. Focus on people's strengths, but help them manage their weaknesses.

Too often it seems that society is conditioned to find the things that are wrong with people versus the special talents and greatness that each person embodies. If you have an employee who writes very well but struggles with public speaking, it is recommended that the leader encourage the employee to continue to improve on that exceptional writing skill. In fact, seek out that employee to proofread some of your memos or advise on articulating an e-mail. The employee will feel important that he or she is not only noticed by the leader of the team, but also being utilized in a capacity above and beyond the job description (helping the boss write clearly and effectively).

Does this mean we encourage the employee to avoid public speaking at all costs? No, that is not what leaders do. Instead, help the employee manage their weakness. For example, if you have an employee who gets extremely nervous at public speaking and gets butterflies a few minutes before presenting, perhaps recommend to the employee to manage that issue. Here are four ways to manage that nervous public speaking issue:

A. At the very beginning of your presentation have a hand-out. Introduce yourself, but then take the next thirty to sixty seconds to walk around and give a hand-out. Oftentimes, this thirty to sixty seconds is all someone needs to calm down and get comfortable.

B. Ask for a quick poll or show of hands regarding something to do with your presentation. The question can be an easy layup or obvious showing of hands, but it gets the audience engaged and gives the speaker a few moments to ask a light, easy question and maybe a comment or two about how many hands went up. Again, sometimes all it takes is a minute to calm the nerves.

C. Tell a quick joke, or something funny that happened that morning. The joke should be quick, light, and just funny enough to loosen up the crowd. Then pivot to a quick overview of who you are and your role in the company. This will buy you enough time to relax and calm the nerves.

D. Take a minute to discuss your experience in preparing for this presentation. The audience will appreciate something unique you stumbled on or something interesting that popped up in the preparation. For example, "You know when I was first asked to give this presentation I had no idea how much I would learn about myself and the passion that I have for this topic . . . Well, let me tell you this has been an eye-opening and rewarding . . . "

Each of these suggestions will not solve your nervous public speaking condition, but will serve as simple and easy ways for you <u>to manage the issue</u> and keep the conversation on "safe mode" until you calm down.

2. Don't just notice it. Say something!

Remember in level 2 of Maxwell's "5 Levels of Leadership" he talks about how leaders listen, observe, and learn? If you notice that an employee went above and beyond in their call of duty, call them down to the office to let them know you noticed what happened and are proud of those efforts. If possible, "spiff" the employee with a small token of appreciation: a gift card, company apparel, an e-mail copying the employee and HR that will ultimately land in their file. When leaders take the time to listen, observe, and learn, the employees notice that YOU notice. It shouldn't surprise you that they will be inspired to want to do it again.

Here's one way to demonstrate to every employee that the leader is listening, observing, and learning: make it a practice to point out something positive in your employees every day. A simple thumbs-up, quick e-mail, brief

©Akaranan/Shutterstock.com

comment at their desk; keep it brief and simple. The key is to be diverse and fair to all employees, and not find yourself complimenting the same two people all of the time.

3. Be an example to your employees.

There is nothing more frustrating than being in a retail store and asking an employee where you can find something particular—only to have the employee point in a general direction and then walk away from you. This is very poor customer service and it borders on lack of respect for another human being. A leader can demonstrate to his/her staff that when a customer asks for help, provide the help. For example, do not just point where the section is, but rather walk the customer TO the section or particular area they desire and happily ask "Is this what you were looking for?" Leaders set a vision for how the team, department, company will run, and then they create a culture of employees who live out that vision.

4. Seek leadership development opportunities.

As Maxwell put it, leadership is a lifelong journey. From the minute you become a supervisor, team leader, manager, or boss you have the opportunity to simply make sure everyone does their jobs—or—inspire the team to achieve greatness for the company and for themselves. Inspiration is the key differentiator. For some, leadership comes natural. But leadership can be developed through education, mentoring, observation, training, and practical experience. In other words, don't just learn about it, but actually put the leadership behaviors into practice. In time, these leadership skills will sharpen and your development will take a natural course.

©nasirkhan/Shutterstock.com

THREE WAYS YOU CAN SEEK LEADERSHIP DEVELOPMENT OPPORTUNITIES

1. Attend leadership conferences and seminars. Visit with your supervisor about leadership seminar opportunities. When in doubt, most municipalities have free or very inexpensive entities such as the local business Chamber of Commerce. The local Chambers of Commerce almost always have leadership seminars. Don't wait to get invited, go get yourself involved!

2. Ask your superior if you can occasionally fill in while he/she is gone from the office. Make it clear that your agenda is to simply gain some experience and develop. If the boss is a true leader, they will not be insecure about providing you those opportunities. (However, most employees never think to ask for this opportunity.)

3. Reading makes the mind sharp.

SUGGESTED READING

- ✓ John Maxwell, *5 Levels of Leadership*
- ✓ Peter Drucker, *Management: Tasks, Responsibilities, Practices*
- ✓ Stephen Covey, *The 7 Habits of Highly Successful People*
- ✓ Jack Welch, *Straight From The Gut*
- ✓ Jim Collins, *Good To Great*
- ✓ Dale Carnegie, *How to Win Friends and Influence People*

CHAPTER SUMMARY

Professional sales representatives embody not only the skills necessary to become effective leaders, they utilize and develop these skills and put them into practice. In other words, they walk the walk. And this is one reason why 20 percent of Fortune 500 CEO's come from sales and marketing backgrounds.

Managers and leaders differ in that leaders seek to inspire and influence; whereas, managers organize and coordinate the office activities while holding staff accountable. Anybody can become a supervisor, manager, or boss.

©EtiAmmos/Shutterstock.com

Leaders are developed and inspire others to expand their horizons. In John Maxwell's *5 Levels of Leadership*, he talks about how a level 1 leader is simply a title person, or an employee with an elevated position. Employees only follow level 1 leaders because of their title. However, as the leader develops and advances through the various levels we begin to see employees who feel respected, listened to, and inspired to do more. The take-away from Maxwell's *5 Levels of Leadership* is that leaders must continuously develop their leadership skills throughout their lifetime with the ultimate goal of developing others to become leaders.

In this chapter we discussed various methods for you to begin working on leadership skills right now. For example, help people identify what they are good at while managing the areas of weakness. If an employee is a good writer but a poor public speaker, help the employee focus on the writing skills. Additionally, leaders listen, observe, and learn. If you hear an employee going above and beyond, take the time to point out that you noticed these efforts. Odds are, the employee will want you to notice again and again.

Leaders live by example. They practice what they preach. Living by example is one way to show leadership in our personal lives and our business. Lastly, take the time to invest in leadership development. Ask your superior for opportunities to hone these skills. Attend conferences and seminars when the company allows, but if they do not offer these opportunities your local business community (Chamber of Commerce) almost always offers leadership development opportunities. The authors listed several leadership and management books that are world-renowned. Make it a personal goal to read at least one book from that list.

REFERENCES

Maxwell, J. C. 2011. *The 5 Levels of Leadership*. New York: Center Street.

Savitz, Eric. 2011. "The Path to Becoming a Fortune 500 CEO." *Forbes* (Dec. 5). https://www.forbes.com/sites/ciocentral/2011/12/05/ the-path-to-becoming-a-fortune-500-ceo/#771d0ce5709b

11 HOMEWORK

Throughout the course we have learned many of the fundamental behaviors and concepts that make up the best sales professionals. Therefore, let us perform an assignment that demonstrates our sales knowledge and perspective.

Assignment

Break up into groups of four to ten (depends on the size of the class). Your group will serve as the corporate sales management team. You are to pick a local business: retail store, car dealership, restaurant, or another business that your professor approves for the purposes of this project.

You are to develop a sales training curriculum for that business and the employees in that business who would need sales training the most. For example, if you choose a restaurant, you would likely target the waitstaff to undergo the corporate sales training program (you may include the hosts and the managers, but you would NOT include the cooks or dishwashers as they do not generally interact with customers).

Once you have broken up into teams, and have selected your business (and selected the department that will need the training the most), you are to deliver a sales training curriculum for that business/department.

What Is a Sales Training Curriculum?

For the purposes of this exercise a sales training curriculum is a "recommended training course." We are not actually providing the training in this exercise, but rather setting up the course, its requirements, and then providing an overview of what the training will entail to the other students in the classroom. (Think of it like this: you outline the courses, select action items for each of those courses, and then you share the course concepts with your students in a presentation near the end of the course. You are NOT providing actual training at this time.)

The presentation should be performed near the end of the course, and should include the entire class to observe. The presentation should be no more than eight to twelve minutes in length, and it should outline the three to five areas of sales training that your corporate sales team has deemed the most critical. For example, you may recommend "Sales Etiquette 101" as one course in your sales training. Sales Etiquette 101 may include action items (or content) covering proper dress code, setting expectations with customers, customer service, and any other areas of basic sales etiquette that the corporate sales team deems critical for the department. Another example of a sales training course could be "Closing the Deal." Many times we have customers who cannot make up their mind about buying. "Closing the Deal" training may help a sales department ask more effective questions, assist employees with overcoming objections, asking the customers for the business, and more.

Other helpful curriculum topics may include networking, positioning, prospecting, and building rapport. (For the purpose of this exercise and this course, the authors recommend building no more than three to five areas of sales training. And then pitch your idea to the class near the end of the course.)

Your professor will provide additional guidelines and expectations.

APPENDIX

THE ART OF SALES COMPETITION

More than seventy universities from several countries participate in sales tournaments known as "Role-Play." The National Collegiate Sales Competition (NCSC) and International Collegiate Sales Competition (ICSC) are the two largest in the United States, and both tournaments have greatly influenced how many of the smaller regional tournaments are organized.

While the judges and scoring will always remain subjective, here are four tips that will undeniably help your sales team prepare for these highly competitive role-play competitions:

1. Introduction

2. Listen/Needs Assessment

3. Sell/Presentation

4. Close

If your team builds their script around these four categories, they will likely impress the judges and hiring companies. Let us walk through each one:

©iQoncept/Shutterstock.com

Introduction (first 60–90 seconds)

Most role-play competitions are allotted 20 minutes for the student to make the sale. While the introduction is usually 5–10 percent of the weighted scoring, and only 60–90 seconds in length, this is arguably the most significant section. How you walk into the room, the clothing you are wearing, the handshake, building rapport, and so forth, all set the tone for the meeting **and** impacts the judges' attention. Therefore, we recommend that coaches and students work diligently on this specific section! While there are a variety of techniques and factors that go into an effective Introduction, here are the three important criteria that should NOT be overlooked in preparing your opening segment:

1. Dress professionally and show some enthusiasm as you walk into the room. This is the moment in which all of the judges are looking at you but likely have NOT taken any notes or scores just yet.

2. Develop a good rapport/conversation skit that allows you to break the ice with the buyer. Once you come into the room and shake hands with the buyer, the time has come to sit down and exchange pleasantries (or build rapport). So as your team prepares for the Introduction, think of a non-threatening conversation skit that you and a mock buyer could BOTH relate to (some students step outside the box and ask irrational questions such as "Did you see the football game this weekend?" Avoid irrational comments like this because the mock buyer may say to you "I don't watch football." This could be embarrassing. Therefore, develop a relatable topic that every mock buyer can identify with!).

3. A smooth pivot from the Introduction to Listening/Needs Assessment is critical. After 60–90 seconds of pleasant conversation, it is recommended to say something like, "OK, I know we only have about 20 minutes today and that your time is valuable. Do you mind if we dive in and I ask you a few questions?" These two sentences are a "pivot" into the Listening/Needs Assessment phase.

Listen/Needs Assessment (5–8 minutes)

The Listening/Needs Assessment phase is sometimes 25–40 percent of the weighted scoring. A true professional doesn't sell/suggest a product or a service until they have effectively uncovered the buyer's true needs. Consider a mortgage banker: customers come into the bank seeking a home loan. A professional mortgage banker will thoroughly review their financial situation BEFORE recommending a 30-year fixed loan, or a 15-year fixed loan, or no loan at all! Regardless, the only way to make a professional recommendation is to ask the right questions . . . and THEN suggest a solution based off of what you learned about the buyer. In the Listening/Needs Assessment phase we recommend that coaches and role-players consider these three factors:

1. Ask the buyer enough questions that will garner you (the seller) three to five challenges that the buyer is experiencing. For example, let's assume you are selling payroll software. Questions that will help you (the seller) uncover the buyer's needs may include:

    a. "Help me understand the process for how you handle payroll right now. Is it manually recorded on a time card? Or is it a software? Can you tell me a little about your current payroll process? (You may find out that they record everything manually, which could mean that human error and mistakes are a concern to the business owner you are selling to.)

b. "If the IRS came in and audited your files, would it be a challenge for you to locate three to five years of previous financial documents and payroll information? Where do you keep the back-up files in case of a fire or theft? And if the IRS did come, whose responsibility would it be to locate the files and work with the IRS agent? Would that be you?" (These questions can expose the possibility for federal penalties and/or fines. These questions also expose time management and resources. For example, how long would it take a staff member to track down all of the files?)

c. "Can you tell me a little bit about the impact that manually recorded time cards has on employees when mistakes are made? Does this also affect your boss and her schedule? If an employee is accidentally overpaid, do they get mad when you require them to pay you back? (You may find out that there are some angry employees in their company right now.)

By asking effective and targeted questions about their process, procedure, impact on employees, impact on the managers, and impact on the company the seller is setting the stage to articulate why his/her products or services may provide a perfect solution to this business.

2. Once you have asked questions about the process, procedure, and impacts to the business, the authors recommend that you repeat BACK what you heard to the buyer. For example:

a. "Okay, I think I have a clear picture of your process and procedure—as well as impact to the organization. If I am hearing you correctly, you are recording payroll manually. And as the company continues to grow this manual process is becoming more of a risk for human error, financial audits—and, quite frankly—employee morale. There's nothing worse than messing up an employee's check and then having to ask them to fix it with you. Am I hearing you correctly? (Most of the time the buyer will agree with you and say "Yes, that is correct." This affirmation from the buyer allows you—the seller—to recommend solutions in the selling phase.)

3. Now that you have identified the buyer's needs, and repeated BACK what you heard, the time has come to smoothly pivot into the Presentation/Selling phase. Here is one way to smoothly pivot:

a. "Okay Mr. Dietrich, I think we have a clear picture of your business—as well as some areas for potential improvement. Let's take a couple minutes and walk through a few recommendations and potential solutions that could make a positive impact on your business. Does this sound okay?" (You have now set the stage to sell your product or service.)

Sell/Presentation (5–7 minutes)

The Presentation and Sell phase will likely account for 25–40% of the weighted scoring, depending on the tournament. In this phase it is recommended to match the buyer's need with your specific solutions. There are three critical areas to consider in this Presentation/Selling phase:

1. Sell them what they need, not what you have. For example:

   a. "Mr. Dietrich, it's truly impressive what your business has been able to accomplish this past five years. And as your business continues to grow, we believe that ABC Software could potentially be a strategic partner on that journey. Our Phase 1 Payroll and HR software will enable every employee to clock in and out electronically. Additionally, it will allow supervisors and managers—such as yourself—the ability to log in from anywhere by computer, cell phone, or tablet to monitor employee hours, overtime, and Paid Time Off (PTO). Since your company has less than fifteen employees, the first year is only $900." (A common mistake many sales professionals make is trying to sell more than what the client needs. This does not mean you shouldn't expose the buyer to the bells and whistles of ABC software, but the main focus of the presentation should be centered around what they need and not the 100 other services that your company offers.)

2. Engage the buyer. For example:

   a. "Mr. Dietrich, let me show you how slick this software is. Take a look at my cell phone. Go ahead and click the payroll button on the main screen (wait for the buyer to click the button). Now, notice how that brings us to the employee section—or list of employees in the company. Also notice how you can see each employee, each day of the week, how many hours they have worked, and how many days of PTO they have earned. Now here is what is really slick about this software: let's say one of your employees—Bob—wants to request a day off. Bob simply logs in and chooses a day off. As his supervisor or manager, the software automatically sends you the PTO day request. You can approve or deny the day right here on your phone! Isn't that pretty slick and easy? (By getting the buyer to physically see, touch, and experience the product or service, you are subtly removing some of the fears and doubts he/she may have about switching from manual payroll to automated.)

3. Return On Investment (ROI)

   a. In any sales tournament or role-play, it is recommended to prepare to demonstrate the ROI to the buyer. In other words, if this software costs $900 a year, how (specifically) does it improve the owner's business or bottom line. Here are two ways to approach ROI:

      i. "How many times in the last year did you overpay an employee and fail to collect that money back?" (Let's assume the buyer says three times.) "Okay, and each time it happened, approximately how much did you overpay the employee?" (Let's assume the buyer says approximately $150.) "Okay, so in those three instances this cost your company $450. If our software eliminated an average of three overpayment mistakes per year, this savings will pay for half the cost of the software."

      ii. In each of those three instances where you overpaid, did it take time out of your day to address the issue with the employee and your boss? (Let's assume the buyer says approximately two hours.) "Okay, so you spent approximately six hours out of your schedule this year addressing mistakes on time cards. If you had those six hours back, is there something around the office that could use those six hours of your time?" (More than likely the buyer will explain where that time could have been better served.)

iii. "If the IRS did audit you, and you could not produce three to seven years of accounting records, did you know that the average fine for a business your size could be anywhere between $2,000–$5,000? Would that be a problem in a small business like yours?"

Pivot smoothly to the close! "Okay Mr. Dietrich. In our meeting today you informed me of five situations in which manually recording Payroll and HR is becoming more of a risk to your company. If ABC Payroll and Software could solve these issues, and almost pay for itself with the ROI we discussed, is there a reason we would not consider moving forward with this conversation?" (You are now set to ask for the business.)

Close (3–4 minutes)

Closing is a critical phase in a sales tournament, and even though this section usually accounts for 15–25 percent, if you fail to close you are almost guaranteed tournament elimination. There are a couple moving parts to the closing section: (1) the time remaining, and (2) the difference between "closing the deal" and gaining a "commitment."

Remember, students only have 20 minutes in a role-play. By the time you enter the Closing phase there are (likely) only a few minutes remaining—assuming you have managed your time very well in the three other phases.

**There is nothing more discouraging than hearing the 20-minute alarm go off and the competitor has failed to earn a commitment from the buyer or "close."

Depending on the role-play skit, you will be either asked to close the deal (which means get a signature and/or contract)—or—gain a commitment (permission to continue the discussion another day or time). It is recommended that students entering the role-play sales competitions set a "closing" or "gain a commitment" as a major objective of competing. In other words, go in prepared to ask for the business—or—at the least an opportunity to escalate the presentation to the decision-maker. If you fail to close or gain a commitment, you will likely not advance to the next round.

ADVICE FOR HANDLING OBJECTIONS

Role-play competitions are designed to have "staged" objections in every round. Objections can run the gamut, but here are five traditional objections you will experience 90 percent of the time:

- ✓ a buyer who talks too much (be careful; these "talkers" will run out your 20 minutes)
- ✓ a buyer who is too busy (stern personality—hard to hold a conversation with)
- ✓ a buyer who is NOT the decision-maker (often making it hard to close the deal)
- ✓ a buyer who is distracted and not paying attention to you (the seller)
- ✓ a buyer who doesn't understand how your product or service will work (disrupt their firm)

Remember this rule: objections are staged and meant to rattle you or disrupt your sales pitch. It is your job to not only prepare for such objections, but to get PAST the objections. Here is how you can prepare:

For a buyer who is too busy, talks too much, or is distracted, we recommend you say something like, "Mr. Dietrich, you had said earlier that we only have 20 minutes today. Why don't we take these 20 minutes and talk about your business, and see if there are solutions that could potentially make an impact on your company?" Many times, simply addressing the objection straight on will lead to the buyer agreeing that the time is short and he/she will no longer "object."

For a buyer who objects because he/she is NOT the decision-maker, we recommend saying something like, "Mr. Nichols, you had said earlier that your firm is experiencing three serious issues. And you agreed that our ABC software solutions would potentially be a great match. Therefore, don't you feel that your boss, Ms. Smith, should have an opportunity to weigh in and ask a few questions? Why don't we set up a meeting with you, Ms. Smith, and myself for Tuesday and get her perspective on these payroll issues?"

For a buyer who objects because they cannot understand how your product or service implementation will not disrupt their business, we recommend ensuring that your company provides adequate training and a 24-7 helpline, if possible. In other words, the seller's company will take care of the implementation process. Also, make it known that you have similar clients, and those clients will serve as a reference for how smooth implementation was for their company. For example, if it is a dentist's office you are selling to, say, "We represent fifteen OTHER dentists in this city, and I have three of them who will serve as a reference if it will help you become more comfortable with our implementation process."

INDEX

F

Face-to-face, 81, 92
Fear, 72
Ford, Henry, 185
Fork in the road, 160
Franklin, Benjamin, 175

G

Goal
    relatability and, 15
    trust and, 15
Going deep level of trust, 13–14
Goman, Carol, 48
Google, 104

H

Hierarchy of communication skills, 81
Homework
    clients for life, 183
    closing the deal, 169
    customer, knowing, 111
    effective communication, 95–96
    listening, 39
    networking and prospecting, 75–76
    objection, 131
    positioning, 147
    sales etiquette, 55
    sales training curriculum, 195–196
    trust and relatability, 21
Honesty, 6, 12
How to Win Friends and Influence People, 80

I

Industry committees, 64–65
Industry knowledge, 100–102
Industry research, 101
Influencer, 104

Influentials, 88
Intelligence Quotient (IQ), 87
International Collegiate Sales Competition
    (ICSC), 197
Introduction, role-play, 197, 198

J

Jefferson, Thomas, 77
Jerry Maguire, 41, 44

L

Leadership, 187–192
    defined, 187
    development opportunities for, 191, 192
    exercise, 188
    five levels of, 187–188
Leadership development opportunities, 191, 192
Level-setting, 102–103
Levitt, Theodore, 115
Lifetime value of customer, 174–175
Likeability, 15, 176
Lincoln, Abraham, 86
LinkedIn, 104
Listening, 24–37
    active, 29–30
    with body, 28–29
    defined, 24
    distraction and, 31
    with ears, 27, 29
    to employees, 85–86
    ethics and, 30–31
    with eyes, 27–28, 29
    homework, 39
    importance of in professional selling, 26
    with mind, 28, 29
    ways to improve skills for, 32–36
Listening/needs assessment, 197, 198–199
Loyalty, 9
Luntz, Frank, 23

M

Management, 186
Maxwell, John, 187, 192
Maxwell's 5 levels of leadership, 187–191, 193
Mind, listening and, 28, 29
Miscommunication, 81

N

National Collegiate Sales Competition (NCSC), 197
Need objection, 126–127, 130
Negativity, 50, 53
Negotiation, 161–163
NetSuite, 70
Networking, 60–74
   defined, 62
   ethics and, 69–70
   event, 61, 65–66
   fear of, 72
   homework, 75–76
   with purpose, 63
   referrals and, 72–73
   ways for, 64–67
   wish list for, 64
New-task buying situation, 81
New task purchasing, 120–122
Non-verbal communication, 90–91

O

Objection, 117–130
   ethics and, 127–128
   homework, 131
   need, 126–127
   price, 124–125
   product, 129
   reasons for, 118–123
   in role-play competition, 201–202
   sales objection defined, 117
   time, 125
Obtaining a commitment, 153–154
ODRE process, 34–36

Open question, 34, 34–35
Operational counseling, 141
Overdelivering, 50–51

P

Parallel the client, 123
Partner, 65
People development leadership level, 187, 188
Performance Improvement Plan (PIP), 87
Permission leadership level, 187, 188
Phone calling, 81
Pine, Karen, 156
Pinnacle leadership level, 187, 188
Political counseling, 141
Poorly-scripted value proposition, 68
Positioning, 136–146
   ethics and, 144–145
   homework, 147
   operational counseling and, 141
   political counseling and, 141
   repetition and, 138–140
   sales, 137
   thought leader and, 141–142
   top of mind positioning and, 142–143
Position leadership level, 187, 188
Price, 160–161
Price objection, 124–125, 130
Probing question, 34–36, 36
   defined, 36
Production leadership level, 187, 188
Product objection, 129, 130
Professional selling
   defined, 4
   importance of listening in, 26
Prospect, ranking by importance, 71
Prospecting, 60–74
   defined, 62
   ethics and, 69–70
   fear of, 72
   with purpose, 63
   referrals and, 72–73
   ways for, 64–67
   wish list for, 64

Q

Qualtrics, 105
Questions, 34–36, 102–103

R

Reflective question, 34
Referral, 72–73, 118
    defined, 72
Reflective question, 34, 35
Relatability, 15–20
    case discussion, 16–18
    defined, 15
    exercise, 18, 20
    homework, 21
    likeability and, 15
    preparation and, 18–19
Repetition, 91, 138–140
Research, industry, 101
Response, 87
Retention. *see* Client retention
Return on investment (ROI), 70
Rogers, Roy, 59, 62
Role play, 8–9
Role-Play competition, 197
    tips for preparing for, 197–201
Role-play sales tournament, 197

S

Sales cycle, 121
Sales etiquette, 42–53
    clarity and concision, 44–46
    compliments and, 48–50
    defined, 44
    ethics and, 51–52
    eye contact, 47–48
    homework, 55
    recommendations and suggestions, 47
    underpromising and overdelivering, 50–51
    ways to improve, 44–51

SalesForce.com, 70
Sales objection, 117
Sales positioning, 137. *see also* Positioning
Sell/presentation, 197, 199–201
    7%–38%–55% rule, 90
Skype, 81
Social events
        networking and, 65
        prospecting and, 65
Strengths, 189
Strong negotiator, 163
Substitution, 91
Sun Tzu, 133
Survey Monkey, 105

T

Target audience. *see* Audience, targeting and
        positioning
Text, 81
Thought leader, 141–142
Time, for sales calling, 106
Time objection, 125, 130
Tone, 90, 92
Top of mind positioning, 142–143
Transactional level of trust, 12–13, 14
Trust, 4–20
    altruism and, 9
    credentials and, 9–10
    defined, 4
    dependability and, 7–9
    ethics and, 6–12
    5 ways to earn in relationship, 5–6
    homework, 21
    levels of, 12–14
    loyalty and, 9
    relatability and, 15–20
    role play, 8–9
Trust levels, 12–14
    exercise, 14
    going deep, 13–14
    transactional, 12–13
Truthfulness, 5–6

U

Underpromising and overdelivering, 50–51
Up communication, 84

V

Value proposition, 67–68
    defined, 67
    exercise, 68
    poorly-scripted example of, 68
    well-scripted example of, 68
Vision, 70
Visuals, 118
Volunteering, 66–67

W

Weak negotiator, 162
Weaknesses, 189
Welch, Jack, 192
Well-scripted value proposition, 68
Word-of-mouth strategy, 118–119

Z

Zellweger, Renee, 44
Ziglar, Zig, 97